At Issue

Does Equality Exist
in America?

Other books in the At Issue series:

Antidepressants
Are America's Wealthy Too Powerful?
Are Conspiracy Theories Valid?
Are Privacy Rights Being Violated?
Child Labor and Sweatshops
Child Sexual Abuse
Creationism Versus Evolution
Does Advertising Promote Substance Abuse?
Does Outsourcing Harm America?
Does the World Hate the United States?
Do Nuclear Weapons Pose a Serious Threat?
Drug Testing
Drunk Driving
The Ethics of Capital Punishment
The Ethics of Genetic Engineering
The Ethics of Human Cloning
Gay and Lesbian Families
Gay Marriage
Gene Therapy
How Can Domestic Violence Be Prevented?
How Does Religion Influence Politics?
Hurricane Katrina
Is American Society Too Materialistic?
Is the Mafia Still a Force in America?
Is Poverty a Serious Threat?
Legalizing Drugs
Natural Disasters
Obesity
Prescription Drugs
Responding to the AIDS Epidemic
School Shootings
Steroids
What Causes Addiction?

At Issue

Does Equality Exist in America?

Stuart A. Kallen, Book Editor

GREENHAVEN PRESS

An imprint of Thomson Gale, a part of The Thomson Corporation

305.0973
DOE

Detroit • New York • San Francisco • New Haven, Conn. • Waterville, Maine • London • Munich

Bonnie Szumski, *Publisher*
Helen Cothran, *Managing Editor*

For more information, contact:
Greenhaven Press
27500 Drake Rd.
Farmington Hills, MI 48331-3535
Or you can visit our Internet site at http://www.gale.com

LIBRARY OF CONGRESS CATALOGING-IN-PUBLICATION DATA

Does equality exist in America? / Stuart A. Kallen, book editor
    p. cm. -- (At issue)
    Includes bibliographical references and index.
    0-7377-3433-7 (lib. : alk. paper) 0-7377-3434-5 (pbk. : alk. paper)
    1. Equality--United States. 2. Marginality, Social--United States 3. Social problems--United States. I. Kallen, Stuart A., 1955– II. Series: At issue (San Diego, Calif.)
    HN90.S6D64 2007
    305.0973--dc22

                                                                    2006043386

Printed in the United States of America
10 9 8 7 6 5 4 3 2 1

Contents

Introduction

The United States is a nation founded on the idea of equal rights as stated in the Declaration of Independence: "We hold these truths to be self-evident, that all men are created equal, that they are endowed by their Creator with certain unalienable rights, that among these are life, liberty and the pursuit of happiness." When the Declaration of Independence was signed in 1776, however, the majority of the Founding Fathers believed that only property-owning, white men should have equal rights, equal access to office, and equal voting power. Women at that time had few political rights, millions of black people were held as slaves, and Native Americans were not considered citizens at all. The inequalities these excluded groups faced created centuries of division and violence that played a large role in American history, from the Civil War to the modern struggle for civil rights. In the twenty-first century, while some argue that all Americans have at last achieved equal rights, others believe that millions of Americans, including women, gays and lesbians, the poor, and other minorities, continue to face inequality.

Proponents of the belief that all Americans have equal rights and opportunities assert that in the United States, anyone who works hard and has drive and ambition can achieve his or her dream. As journalist David Horowitz writes, "The greatest ambition of the civil rights movement has been achieved. The doors of opportunity have been opened and the rules have been made as neutral as they humanly can be to ensure that the competition is fair. . . . The civil war was won. America has outlawed segregation and discrimination. The civil rights cause was victorious. It's time for everyone. . . to move on to more productive debates."

Those who agree with Horowitz often draw upon historical comparisons to make their point. For example, they note that over the past forty years, there has been a dramatic rise in the number of African Americans elected to political office. In 1960, there were about two hundred black politicians in the entire country, most of them in northern states. By 2005, at least eighty-four hundred African Americans were serving in political office, including one senator, forty legislators in the House of Representatives, and more than six hundred African-American legislators in state offices. Gains have also been made by the Hispanic community and other minorities.

Some people argue that equality has been achieved in the workplace as well as in the political world. Since 1965, when Congress passed federal legislation that banned racial and gender discrimination on the job, the number of women and minorities entering the workplace has grown at a rapid pace and transformed American society. For instance, in the 1960s, less than 20 percent of women held jobs, and most worked as secretaries, teachers, or nurses. Women lawyers, doctors, politicians, and corporate executives were extremely rare. Between 1970 and 1990, however, the percentage of women physicians more than doubled—from 7.6 percent to 16.9 percent. In addition, from 1973 to 1993, the percentage of women lawyers and judges jumped from 5.8 percent to 22.7 percent, and the proportion of female engineers grew from 1.3 percent to 8.6 percent. Today, women serve as senior executives at dozens of major corporations, including Bloomingdale's, CBS, Coca-Cola, Disney, DuPont, Southwest Airlines, Home Depot, and Visa.

Although many women and minorities have been able to advance in the political arena and workplace, some experts argue that the United States still does not have widespread equality. They point out that a 2003 survey of Fortune 500 corporations by Catalyst, a New York City–based organization that studies women and business trends, shows that almost 86 percent of senior executives are men. Women, who represent 46 percent of the workforce hold only about 15 percent of the senior-level jobs in major corporations, and only 1.6 percent are women of color.

There are also significant gaps in wages that some say are based on sex and race. Studies show that the average woman makes only 71 cents for every dollar a man makes at a similar job. Black women are paid 63 cents and Hispanic women 54 cents for every dollar men earn in comparable jobs. Moreover, male and female African Americans face much higher rates of unemployment. In December 2005, the national unemployment rate for whites was 3.7 percent, while more than 10 percent of black people were unemployed. In some inner-city neighborhoods, about half of all African Americans who wanted jobs could not find one.

Unemployment and poverty, some argue, remain a large obstacle to achieving equality in America. Author Kenneth L. Karst asserts that a lack of money in modern society limits a person's equal participation in society. In his book *Belong to America*, he writes,

> It takes resources to participate in activities that the community regards as validating—to be an effective husband or wife or parent, for example; to hold a job; or be engaged in some leisure pursuits that command respect. These resources begin with income and assets, but they may also include social contacts or knowledge or political influence or health ... a list notable for its inclusion of things money can buy.

Although few people would argue that the poor in the United States have fewer opportunities than in the 1960s when African Americans were openly denied access to higher education and jobs, many Americans still struggle for access to the equal opportunities promised to them in the Constitution.

Throughout history people have been judged by their skin color, economic class, sex, and other factors. They have faced severe discrimination and lived without the possibility of achieving equal rights and opportunities. The fact that Americans make an effort to address these difficult issues of equality is a sign of hope and progress. The debate over equality in the United States, however, has been one of the most contentious in recent times, and it is doubtful that the arguments will be resolved anytime soon.

1

The United States Is a Land of Equal Opportunity

Walter E. Williams

Walter E. Williams is the author of America: A Minority Viewpoint, All It Takes Is Guts, South Africa's War on Capitalism *and* The State Against Blacks, *later made into a television documentary. He writes a weekly column, "A Minority View," for Heritage Features Syndicate.*

Liberal politicians often complain that the rich have too much money. They forget, however, that the United States is a land of equal opportunity where anyone with a good idea who is willing to work hard may join the ranks of the wealthy. Surveys show that many of today's millionaires came from humble circumstances. Instead of telling the poor that the rich are getting richer at their expense, politicians and pundits should emphasize the message of equality. Through education and sacrifice, anyone willing to strive for success can achieve the American dream.

Let's talk about the rich—those people who, according to former Congressman Richard Gephardt, are "winners in life's lottery." Or the people whom director Michael Moore preaches, in his book *Dude, Where's my Country?* got rich off the backs of the poor.

Farrah Gray was raised in a predominantly black Chicago neighborhood. At age 8, he started a lemonade stand business, later a venture capital business, a food business and a magazine. By age 17, Farrah Gray was a millionaire, had been chief executive of four companies, and had offices on Wall Street, and in Las Vegas and Los Angeles.

While becoming a millionaire by age 17 is rare, eventually becoming a millionaire isn't. According to TNS Financial Services' 2004 Affluent Market Research survey, there are an estimated 8.2 million American households with assets, excluding primary residences, worth over $1 million.

That's a 33 percent increase over the 6.2 million millionaire households in 2003.

---

80 percent of today's American millionaires are first-generation rich.

Who are these people portrayed either as winners in life's lottery or who got rich by exploiting the poor? One thing for sure is that they're not the sons and daughters of [the nation's wealthiest families] the Rockefellers, the Kennedys or the Vanderbilts. According to Drs. Thomas Stanley and William Danko's research published in their book *The Millionaire Next Door: The Surprising Secrets of America's Wealthy*, 80 percent of today's American millionaires are first-generation rich.

Drs. Stanley and Danko listed other characteristics of these 8.2 million millionaire households. Fewer than 20 percent inherited 10 percent or more of their wealth. More than half never received as much as a dollar in inheritance. Fewer than 25 percent received "an act of kindness" from a relative greater than $10,000, and 91 percent never received, as a gift, as much as $1 from the ownership of a family business.

Being first-generation rich is not new for Americans. Drs. Stanley and Danko say, "More than 100 years ago the same was true. In *The American Economy*, [economist] Stanley Lebergott reviews a study conducted in 1892 of the 4,047 American millionaires. He reports that 84 percent were nouveau riche [newly rich], having reached the top without the benefit of inherited wealth."

There is so much economic mobility in our society that starting out with modest means or even being dirt poor does not prevent one from ending up at the top.

This points to one of the most unique features of our nation.

The Politics of Envy

Just because you know where a person ended up in life is no guarantee that you can tell where he started. In other words, there is so much economic mobility in our society that starting out with modest means or even being dirt poor does not prevent one from ending up at the top.

According to IRS tax data, 85.8 percent of tax filers in the bottom fifth in 1979 had moved on to a higher quintile, and often to the top quintile, by 1988.

Here's my question for you: What are we to make of people who preach pessimism and doom to people—telling them that they're poor because others are rich or telling blacks that they'll never make it because of societal racism? What are we to make of politicians, media pundits and college professors who preach the politics of envy—telling people lies that the rich became rich off the backs of the poor? I grew up poor in a housing project in North Philadelphia, and those weren't the lessons prevalent a half-century ago. My mother used to preach that "We have a beer pocketbook but champagne tastes." And my stepfather used to admonish, "If you want to make it in this world, you have to come early and stay late."

Those messages are far more beneficial to a poor person than those of victimhood and pity. Personally, I like evangelical minister Reverend Ike's response when asked what should we do about the poor. He said, "The best thing you can do for the poor is not become one."

2

America's Wealthy Have Unfair Advantages

Charles R. Morris

Charles R. Morris is the author of many books, including American Catholic *and* Money, Greed, and Risk.

Many Americans believe that the United States is a land of equal opportunity but statistics show that this is not true. A small group of extremely wealthy families own nearly two-thirds of the wealth in the United States while the middle class and poor in the past twenty years have seen their incomes stagnate or shrink. Big tax breaks granted to the rich since the 1980s have contributed to the inequality between income groups. Unless the government acts to reverse trends that favor moneyed interests, the gap between rich and poor will continue to grow at unprecedented levels. This will leave America a divided nation where the promise of equality is a faded memory.

America has always had an ambivalent attitude toward equality. In contrast to the social democratic regimes of Europe, the only officially endorsed equality Americans have historically embraced is the narrow sense of equality of opportunity—as opposed to outcome. A suspicion of government interference in economic matters is an attitude that dates from the early days of the republic. When [French author Alexis] de Tocqueville lauded the rough equality of Americans in the 1830s, he made it clear that it is the fluidity

Charles R. Morris, "Economic Injustice for Most: From the New Deal to the Raw Deal," *Commonweal*, vol. 131, August 13, 2004, p. 12–15. Copyright © 2004 Commonweal Publishing Co., Inc. Reproduced by permission of Commonweal Foundation.

of the society that impressed him: "I do not mean that there is any lack of wealthy individuals in the United States. . . . But wealth circulates with inconceivable rapidity, and experience shows that it is rare to find two succeeding generations in the full enjoyment of it."

The richest 1 percent of the population now owns about a third, and the top 5 percent about 58 percent, of all wealth.

[Abraham] Lincoln made much the same point: "[It is] best to leave each man free to acquire property as fast as he can. Some will get wealthy; I don't believe in a law to prevent a man from getting rich [but] . . . we do wish to allow the humblest man an equal chance to get rich with everyone else." Yet the vast accretions of personal fortunes and corporate power that accompanied the rough-and-tumble era of free-booting capitalism in the decades after the Civil War—when men like John D. Rockefeller, Andrew Carnegie, and Jay Gould were building their empires—cast doubt on the reality of the American mythos of equal opportunity.

Carnegie loved to pose as the friend of the workingman, basking in the attendant public applause, until the searing events of the 1892 Homestead strike exposed the savage working conditions at his plants—twelve-hour days, seven-day weeks, a single scheduled day off a year, squalid little company towns, contaminated water, near-starvation wages. (After the strike was broken with much violence, Carnegie salved his conscience and burnished his image by giving the borough of Homestead a library.)

By 1890, at the height of the Gilded Age, just 1 percent of the population owned slightly more than a quarter of all the nation's wealth. That data was reconstructed by historians, but widespread awareness of a growing, and possibly unbridgeable, chasm between the Haves and the Have-Nots fueled the

Populist movement in the last years of the nineteenth century, the Progressive politics and trust-busting initiatives early in the twentieth, and Franklin Roosevelt's New Deal. After World War II, and through the 1950s and 1960s, there was substantial leveling of wealth and income. The rich were still very rich, but programs like the G.I. Bill [which provided college tuition for returning World War II veterans] restored the conviction that the ladder Americans had to climb to attain real wealth evidenced the scale of the opportunity rather than the height of the barriers.

The current patterns of income concentration are violently out of whack with historical experience, and may indeed be without precedent.

Virtually all those gains have been dissipated over the past twenty-five years or so. Instead of controlling a quarter of the nation's wealth, as in the Gilded Age, the richest 1 percent of the population now owns about a third, and the top 5 percent about 58 percent, of all wealth. Those numbers represent the densest concentration of wealth since the peak of American wealth inequality, which was in 1929, a not entirely reassuring precedent.

The Trends

The recent trends in income concentration have been even more pronounced than those in wealth. This is unusual and especially worrisome. Wealth accumulations occur over extended periods, so it can take a number of years for even highly skewed income patterns to be fully reflected in wealth distributions. The current patterns of income concentration are violently out of whack with historical experience, and may indeed be without precedent.

If we divide wage earners into five quintiles—from the bottom fifth through the top fifth—over the period from 1980 though 2001, every quintile but the top one saw its share of the national income pie shrink—that is, not just the poor and the lower-middle classes, but the middle classes and the upper-middle classes also. Predictably, the poorest quintile took the biggest hit, with the blow softening as one moves up the income ladder.

At the household level, total incomes barely kept pace with inflation in the lower quintiles. The annual improvement was about half a percent a year in the lowest quintile, a bit more than eight-tenths of a percent a year for the middle class, and just about 1 percent a year for the upper-middle class. Even in the top quintile, the gains were highly concentrated in the top 5 percent. And note too that these are household incomes. Average real wages for all production workers actually dropped about half a percent a year over this period, so most households were able to stay even only by putting more of their members to work. The real income of full-time year-round male workers has been essentially unchanged in thirty years. (Full-time, year-round female workers have seen a strong earnings rise, though from a much lower base.)

Shocking? Well it gets worse. Over the thirty years from 1970 to 2000, the bottom 90 percent of earners as a group actually lost ground. All the top 10 percent did well, but only the top 1 percent did extremely well, and even within the top 1 percent gains were disproportionately concentrated within the top hundredth of 1 percent, a mere 13,400 households.

If you read the financial news, you know that the period from 1980 through 2001 marked one of the greatest of American economic booms—when we recovered our competitive position in the world, and created entirely new high-technology industries. Well, guess who reaped all the gains from that hard work? Almost all the benefits flowed to the very rich. The poor, the lower-middle class, the middle class, even the upper-middle class, got almost nothing at all. So much for fairy tales about rising tides.

What Happened?

The truth is that the amazing spurt in top-drawer incomes is so sudden, so striking, so out of keeping with experience, that it will take economists years to reach a consensus on the details of what happened, if they ever do. But there are some obvious factors at work.

The 1986 Tax Reform Act was a signal nonpartisan accomplishment, worked out between the Reagan administration and a substantially Democratic tax-reform wing of the Congress, led notably by Senator Bill Bradley. The core principle of the reform was to trade a greatly simplified tax code, eliminating almost all special privileges and shelters, for an extraordinary, across-the-board reduction in tax rates and the number of brackets. As far as possible, all income was to be treated alike—there was to be no difference in the taxation of capital gains [income earned: from stocks or property] and ordinary income, no difference between the [business owners] and the ordinary wage earner. Although the act was sometimes blamed for the era's large deficits, an IRS analysis showed that tax receipts actually increased the year after its passage.

Sadly, almost as soon as it was passed, tax advocates for the wealthy began lobbying for a restoration of special tax breaks, especially in the treatment of capital gains. (Taxable capital gains, of course, accrue almost entirely to the wealthy. The current tax exclusion for capital gains on the sale of a home—$500,000 for a couple—effectively eliminates taxes on the vast majority of home sales, while the stocks and bonds owned by ordinary people are mostly in pension funds and 401(k) plans, which are already tax-protected.) By the time the capital gains tax preference was finally restored, in complicated horse-trading with an embattled Clinton administration in 1998, most of the other shelters that benefit the very rich had wormed their way back into the code also. Although there were modest increases in the top rates under the first President Bush and President Bill Clinton, actual tax rates paid by top-tier earners stayed flat or fell, even as their incomes steadily rose.

A second factor was a devastating campaign of vilification against the Internal Revenue Service by the [Congressman] Newt Gingrich wing of the Republican Party. A thoroughly cowed agency drastically reduced its auditing activities to the point where the working poor—who can receive a maximum $4,120 benefit under the Earned Income Tax Credit—were more likely to be audited than substantial small businesses, and three times more likely than individuals earning more than $100,000. By all reports tax evasion has soared, as evidenced by the aggressive marketing of illegal tax shelters by some of our most august financial institutions.

The almost inconceivable leap in executive income has naturally stimulated a free-for-all rush for even more tax privileges and shelters.

There was also an extraordinary outbreak of greed on the part of Wall Street executives and business leaders. By 1999, the average pay of the 100 top CEOs was $37 million. Between 1970 and 2000, the average American worker's paycheck improved by about $2 a week each year, mostly resulting from gains made by women. At the same time, CEO pay improved $26,000 a week each year—every year for thirty years. The almost inconceivable leap in executive income has naturally stimulated a free-for-all rush for even more tax privileges and shelters—special treatment for stock options, offshore hedge funds, companies paying for personal expenses, tax benefits for owning corporate jets, and many, many more. That such unseemly looting has become socially acceptable, not to say praiseworthy, is an inquiry for social psychology, not economics.

Finally, it is worth noting that virtually all these data are from the period before the [2003] Bush administration tax cuts on capital gains, stock dividends, and estate taxes. Taken together, the Bush program will beam the very rich out to new galaxies of wealth far, far, away from the rest of us. The single-mindedness with which the administration has focused on benefits for the narrow band of the super-rich is astonishing. Congressional Democrats, for example, have proposed raising the ceiling on the estate tax to $4 million, or a similarly high figure, rather than totally eliminating it. The administration responds with ritual denunciations of "death taxes" on "small businesses" and "family farmers." In fact, the most recent data on average estates at death show that for people in the 99–99.5th percentile of income, the average estate was only about $2.1 million. The big winners from the Bush program are our 13,400 friends in the top .01 percent whose average estate was about $87 million. This is a tax platform that would make Louis XIV proud.

Why Should We Care?

The problem is not that some people are getting rich. Lincoln was right that the fluidity and mobility of America make up a great part of its attraction. But there are many problems with developing a class of super-rich. For one thing, as the tiering of American wealth distribution stretches further and further upward, it reduces mobility. The children of the poor now disproportionately stay poor, to an extent far beyond any explication based on lower intelligence or race, while the children of the rich disproportionately stay rich, again to an extent that can't be explained by their talent or IQs. There is also substantial evidence that a number of other developed countries—including Germany, Canada, Sweden, and Finland—now have more social mobility than America does. The justification for policies that mildly even out wealth accumulation is much like those for regulating business competition.

Americans are in favor of free competition and applaud the winners, but we also believe that it is right to step in to level the playing field when competition ends in monopoly.

3

American Minorities Enjoy the Same Opportunities as Whites

Armstrong Williams

Armstrong Williams is a conservative political commentator, newspaper columnist, and daily talk show host.

African Americans have more opportunities today than at any other time in history. While old guard liberal activists continue to blame white racism for problems in minority communities, they ignore the remarkable gains made by African Americans since the 1960s. Today, many young black people have the same aspirations and ideals as young whites and are equally able to achieve their dreams. Instead of focusing on past discrimination, African American leaders must realize that social and economic limits are no longer imposed because of the color of a person's skin. It is the tendency to play the victim and blame others that holds back black people in a land of equal opportunity.

President [George W.] Bush's [2004] inaugural address . . . was studded with grand ideas about spreading freedom and democracy throughout the world. The event coincided with the anniversary of Dr. Martin Luther King's birthday [January 15], raising the question of how close we have come to fulfilling that dream here at home.

So, how stands this country now, more than three decades after Dr. King gave his life for his dream? Certainly, there has been a progression from the days when those blacks who demanded freedom from oppression were made to fear for their lives.

The racism of today isn't so blunt as to be about skin color. Rather, it is about cultural patterns that slavery wrought. It is about cultural division that was sewn so deeply into our social fabric, for so long, that even today white Americans have trouble imagining themselves as the "other" skin color. In short, modern racism is about elitism and a lack of empathy.

Blaming All Problems on Racism

The response of black leaders has understandably been one of anger and separatism. Early leaders of the civil rights movement settled on the theory that American society was primarily characterized by racism and that American institutions were grounded in the maintenance of racial privilege.

Many of the black politicians who swept into office on the heels of the movement consciously embodied this organizing principle. Their legislative remedies were predicated on the belief that the problems of black people—whether high crime rates, drug use or poor educational performance—were primarily, if not entirely, the result of white racism.

Their obligation was to promote and protect their constituents by offering remedies to specific aspects of racial discrimination—such as segregated schools, disparity in pay, public accommodations, etc. In other words, they wed their legitimacy to the belief that all of the problems confronting blacks were rooted in racism.

Liberal black officeholders ... underplay the dramatic improvements in economic and social status experienced by blacks over the last 40 years.

To this day, many liberal black officeholders depend on the perception of ongoing, widespread racism in order to remain competitive in the electoral process. They underplay the dramatic improvements in economic and social status experienced by blacks over the last 40 years. Large numbers of their constituents—particularly those who came to age during the overt racism of the past half-century—continue to believe that the problems confronting the black lower class stem primarily from racism.

Herein lies the greatest missed opportunity of the civil rights movement: They never prepared for the day when whites would start treating minorities as equals. Their entire public image—their very legitimacy as political and cultural spokespersons—was predicated on the rhetoric of a black-versus-white war. As Justice Clarence Thomas once observed, "The [civil rights] revolution missed a larger point by merely changing the status [of minorities] from invisible to victimized."

An Optimistic Outlook

In recent years, however, a younger generation of black Americans, whose political and social attitudes were not shaped by civil rights struggle, has begun to move beyond the notion that race is an ongoing problem that handicaps all blacks everywhere. This younger generation has no personal experience with legal segregation and "Jim Crow" laws. They have not been treated as second-caste citizens, or conditioned to hate themselves.

Lacking the psychic scars of their parents and grandparents, they are more optimistic about the idea—and the reality—of being part of the middle class. According to the Joint Center for Political and Economic Studies, young black professionals from ages 18 to 34 are more optimistic about their career prospects (81.8 percent) than either the baby boomers (66.8 percent) or those over age 50 (58.2 percent).

Yes, they are aware of race, but they also have a keen sense of future possibilities—much more so than did their parents and grandparents.

These differences in perspective are manifesting themselves in seismic shifts in public opinion. For example, there no longer exists much difference between what young black Americans and white Americans rate as their top priority concerns. According to a recent Joint Center study, each group ranked education, health care, crime and the economy among its top five areas of concern.

Young black Americans are no longer willingly isolating themselves from mainstream society along the fault line of black and white issues.

That marks a profound change. Young black Americans are no longer willingly isolating themselves from mainstream society along the fault line of black and white issues. They want issues-oriented solutions, not racial rhetoric. That spells profound changes not just for the black political landscape but also for the entire national dialogue.

Opposition from the Old Guard

In political races across the country, these generational shifts are coming into focus. There are a number of new-wave moderate and conservative black political leaders gaining local and state offices who are not connected to the liberal Democratic black establishment. Elected leaders like Kent Williams, Cory Booker, Harold Ford Jr., Kwame Kilpatrick and others are articulating a new vision and agenda.

These new leaders are more conservative than the old guard. They tend to be less certain that racism is the prime reason for the lack of progress among many blacks. Most oppose race-based affirmative action. Unlike the old guard, they do not see America as being fundamentally flawed because of its unfortunate racial history or its capitalist economic system.

They are more inclined to encourage choice and market-based approaches, such as school vouchers and black entrepreneurship.

Sadly, they are facing stiff opposition not only from Democrats but also from the old guard of civil rights leaders who are fearful of falling into irrelevancy. Discrimination and victimhood form the foundation upon which they have built their legitimacy as our representatives. They cannot embrace a new covenant because they have sacrificed everything to the old ones.

More and more black Americans are coming to the conclusion that liberalism has not solved our most basic problems.

Moving Beyond Liberalism

Their response has been one of panic. They do everything they can to drum the new wave of black conservatives out of the black community. But things are changing. More and more black Americans are coming to the conclusion that liberalism has not solved our most basic problems. Instead, it has put us in the mindset that we have to be fed government programs instead of being given access to capital and the opportunity to create our own jobs.

This younger generation of black Americans is saying it is time to move beyond the basic covenants of liberalism and finally face who we are and what we need, not solely as blacks, but as individuals.

This is a good thing. Instead of coming together in order that we might be one with the Democrats, I say let us separate and vote and live as individuals, aware of race and its implications in our society, but also capable of expressing our individual wants and needs.

Therein lies the true hope for equality.

4

American Minorities Do Not Enjoy the Same Opportunities as Whites

Betsy Leondar-Wright et al.

Betsy Leondar-Wright is coauthor of the books The Color of Wealth *and* Class Matters *and communications director for United for a Fair Economy, a national organization founded to raise awareness about the issue of concentrated wealth and power. Meizhu Lui is the executive director of United for a Fair Economy and coauthor of the book* The Color of Wealth. *Gloribell Mota is the Fair Taxation Educator at United for a Fair Economy. Dedrick Muhammad is the former coordinator of the Racial Wealth Divide Project of United for a Fair Economy and executive director of Global Justice. Mara Voukydis is a researcher with United for a Fair Economy's Racial Wealth Divide Project.*

Conservative politicians often promote the concept of an ownership society, based on the idea that all Americans should take personal responsibility for their health care, education, housing, and retirement with limited government assistance or interference. However, most African Americans and other minorities have been shut out of the ownership society because they lack equal access to jobs, housing, and business opportunities. Instead of living in an ownership society where everyone has access to the American Dream, people of color find themselves in a divided nation where the desires of the rich are given greater government priority than the needs of the poor.

After steady gains in the 1990s, African Americans, Latinos, and other people of color financially stagnated or lost ground during the first term of President [George W.] Bush. Without a dramatic change in policy more of the same can be expected. Even . . . years after the 2001 recession, the latest economic indicators point to Blacks and Latinos disproportionately suffering under "compassionate conservatism," which thus far has conserved this country's racial wealth divide. . . .

A committed president must take into account our history of racial privilege and must acknowledge, in pushing for an Ownership Society, the complexity of broadening the scope of ownership for *all* Americans.

This second annual [2005] report points out that today's Ownership Society disowns too many Americans along racial lines. This report also offers a range of federal strategies, the community empowerment programs needed to bring them to life, and the tax policies needed to fund them. . . .

Throughout US history, steady jobs with good pay have been held primarily by white people, leaving all groups of color with high poverty and unemployment rates.

Barriers to Owning Assets

Ownership of assets depends on a steady income higher than the cost of living. Only with a living wage can a family build up a savings account, start a business, put a down payment on a house, pay a mortgage, or maintain property. Throughout US history, steady jobs with good pay have been held primarily by white people, leaving all groups of color with high poverty and unemployment rates.

America has always been an Ownership Society—for white men. For long periods of its history, non-white racial groups were prevented from owning assets, and African Americans were actually owned as assets.

After steady gains, we have seen Blacks and Latinos lose jobs and income [since 2001]. . . . A true Ownership Society would mean reversing this trend so that full employment is the norm and all working people make enough to save. The US economy moved in that direction between 1988 and 2000, but much of that progress has been lost.

Unemployment

"When there is massive unemployment in the black community, it is called a social problem. But when there is massive unemplyoment in the white community, it is called a depression."

—*Dr. Martin Luther King*

The 2001 recession was followed by the first jobless recovery since the Great Depression. After the recession during President Bush, Sr.'s administration [1988–1992] both Black and Latino unemployment rates fell below their pre-recession levels within two years. But we have yet to see a similar decrease in unemployment for Blacks and Latinos in the post-recession economy since 2001.

Federal policies contributed to this jobless recovery. The three major tax cuts from 2001 to 2004 widened the racial income divide by targeting high-income taxpayers, who are disproportionately white. The previous three Congresses and administrations, both Democratic and Republican, responded to recessions with more proactive policies aimed at getting people back to work.

The African American unemployment rate fell steadily from 1988 to 2000, except for a spike around the 1992 recession. In 2000 it reached a historic low of 7.1%. It rose above 10% in January 2002, and has stayed between 9.9% and 12% ever since. Latino/Hispanic unemployment rates also dropped from 8% in 1988 to 5.7% in 2000, but rose again in the last four years.

These numbers are, of course, only the official unemployment rate. Discouraged workers and others not in the labor force are not included. As of November 2004, 36% of Black adults, 32% of Latino adults, and 34% of white and Asian adults were not in the labor force.

The growing numbers of people of color in prison also don't count as unemployed. At the end of 2003, of the 1.4 million people sentenced to more than a year in prison, about 44% were African American, 19% were Latino, and 35% were white. The Justice Department estimates that if current trends continue, almost a third of black men, over a sixth of Latino men and one in twenty white men will enter state or federal prison in their lifetimes.

State Budget Cuts Hurt Minorities

During the economic downturn of 2001, state spending fell from over 5% of the Gross Domestic Product to 4.6%. State spending has not returned to its 1990s average of 4.85% despite three years of recovery.

While the recession and state tax cuts are certainly the immediate causes of the drop in state spending, the federal government's reluctance to help states with their fiscal crises also played a role. In an ironic coincidence, the Bush administration's 2002–2004 tax cuts gave the wealthiest 1% (overwhelmingly white) almost exactly the same amount of money as the deficits of all 50 states in the same three years— $197.3 billion compared with $200 billion.

This political choice had racial implications. Public services are disproportionately used by people of color. When Georgia cuts pregnant women and infants off Medicaid, when Florida and Massachusetts reduce child care subsidies, when California, Maryland and Texas spend less on public higher education, low and moderate-income people of color are overrepresented among the people harmed.

Income and Poverty

"I must return to the valley all over the South and in the big cities of the North—a valley filled with millions of our white

>and Negro brothers who are smoldering in an airtight cage of
>poverty in the midst of an affluent society."

>—*Dr. Martin Luther King*

Inadequate income and persistent poverty have always been the most formidable obstacles to asset development for people of color. If every dollar is going to necessities, saving and investing are impossible.

People of color have made great strides in gaining more income over the last two generations, but that progress has recently been eroded. Median income fell for all racial groups during the first Bush administration, but it fell faster for people of color than for white people, widening the racial income gap.

After slowly increasing from 55% of white income in 1988 to 65% in 2000, black median income fell again to 62% in 2003, according to the Census Bureau. Similarly, Latino income rose from 69% to 73% of white income, but then fell back to 69% in 2003. Asian Americans rose as high as 122% of white income in 2000, but had dropped back to 116% by 2003.

About half of the progress in median income from 1996 to 2000 was wiped out in the following three years. African Americans finally broke the $30,000 barrier in 2000, with the typical household getting $31,690, but then lost more than $2,000 by 2003. (All dollar figures are corrected for inflation to be in 2003 dollars.) Latinos and Asians lost even more, about $2,500 and $4,000 respectively. The typical white household lost almost $1,000 in income from 2000 to 2003. . . .

Over 798,000 African American families rose out of poverty between 1992 and 2000, with more than two million children, men and women in those families. Then 300,000 families dropped below the poverty line from 2000 to 2003.

Latino poverty is more complicated, as waves of new immigrants arrived at various points. New immigrants tend to be poorer than families already established in the US. There were 385,000 more poor Latinos in 2003 than in 2000, but the connection with policy is less clear.

Many poor people are employed. Black and Latino workers are more likely to be in jobs with pay too low to lift a family of four above the poverty line. Though Latinos make up less than one-seventh of the US workforce, they hold more than one-fifth of the below-poverty-wage jobs. African Americans make up one-ninth of the workforce but hold one-seventh of these low-wage jobs. White Americans, by contrast, make up almost seven-tenths of the workforce, but hold fewer than six-tenths of the low-wage jobs.

An Ownership Society?

"Let us be dissatisfied until those who live on the outskirts of hope are brought into the metropolis of daily security."

—Dr. Martin Luther King

People of color are more likely to be disrupted by economic turmoil because they don't have enough assets to protect them during times of unemployment, family responsibilities, illness and disability. A true Ownership Society would give security to those who now lack it.

Fewer than half of Blacks and Latinos, and fewer than 60% of Asians and American Indians own their own homes, compared to three quarters of whites.

But any government or foundation that aims to expand asset ownership needs to understand the deep roots of the current inequality in net worth. Income can change on a dime, but wealth changes over generations. Our lives are shaped by the wealth—or lack of wealth—of our parents, our grandparents and our ancestors. As an estimated 80 percent of assets come from transfers from prior generations, the asset gap is unlikely to be closed quickly.

Homeownership

Homeownership is recognized as the strongest building block of wealth, and thanks in part to record-low interest rates, more people of color own homes now than ever before. A great race gap, however, remains. Fewer than half of Blacks and Latinos, and fewer than 60% of Asians and American Indians own their own homes, compared to three-quarters of whites.

Offering a proactive agenda to increase homeownership for people of color, President Bush has declared homeownership for white Americans and Americans of color alike a requisite of the new Ownership Society. For example, in 2002, he said, "We must begin to close this homeownership gap by dismantling the barriers that prevent minorities from owning a piece of the American dream."

Though his focus on homeownership for people of color has drawn praise, many worry that the agenda is far from adequate.

A number of barriers to homeownership must be addressed by any adminstration that wants to eliminate the homeownership gap. While the median price of homes in America has increased greatly year by year, the median income of Blacks, Latinos, and Native Americans has declined over the past three years, making it harder for them to buy a home.

In addition, high rates of predatory lending and loan rejection for Blacks, Latinos, and Native Americans suggest that, without more direct intervention, the growth in homeownership will not pick up the pace any time soon.

Two long-time commissioners on the US Commission on Civil Rights evaluated Bush's homeownership and housing success in their recent report, "Redefining Rights in America," stating, "The $200 million in federal funding for 40,000 families is too small given that the housing crisis, particularly with respect to blacks, is so chronic and critical."...

Unfortunately, while pursuing his homeownership agenda, Bush has shown little allegiance to low-income tenants, who should also be considered prospective homebuyers. Fair housing advocates and members of Congress defeated a 2005 budget proposal to decrease Section 8 voucher funding by $1 billion, which would have steered hundreds of thousands of low-income tenants, disproportionately people of color, towards homelessness. While an appropriations bill increases voucher spending for 2005, critics insist that the increase does not match the growing expense of rent and utilities.

Homeownership is, on average, a much greater asset for white people than for people of color. The median value of homes owned by Blacks and American Indians is less than 66% of the value of white-owned homes. The median value of Latino-owned homes is 85% that of white-owned homes. . . .

Justice Is Needed

"At a time when older Americans have longer lives and more options than ever before, we need to ensure they have access not just to a monthly check, but to personal wealth. And I mean all Americans—not just a few, but all Americans, especially women and minorities who are often short-changed by the current Social Security system."

—President Bush, Feb 28, 2002

"The agony of the poor impoverishes the rich; the betterment of the poor enriches the rich . . . whatever affects one directly affects all indirectly."

—Dr. Martin Luther King

This report challenges entrenched aspects of our economy that block the dream that our nation celebrates every year. When Martin Luther King traveled to Washington, D.C. in 1963, he didn't go just to tell people about a dream. He went to "cash a promissory note," the promise of life, liberty, and the pursuit of happiness for all found in the Declaration of Independence. This promise cannot be kept without a government commitment to provide some measure of financial opportunity and security for all of us.

Many Americans still suffer from the accumulated effects of the historical exclusion of their people, and barriers to wealth creation persist.

For centuries, vast private wealth was created from government-orchestrated human rights disasters: the African slave trade, the conquest of Mexico and Puerto Rico, and the genocide of indigenous peoples. While this is an uncomfortable topic that most would like to put under "file closed," these government policies left a legacy that is still very much with us today. Many Americans still suffer from the accumulated effects of the historical exclusion of their people, and barriers to wealth creation persist.

In 1967 Dr. King addressed the Southern Christian Leadership Conference by saying, "Your whole structure must be changed. A nation that will keep people in slavery for 244 years will thingify them—make them things. Therefore they will exploit them, and poor people generally, economically. . . . What I am saying today is that we must go from this convention and say, America, you must be born again!"

America must be born again with new values, values that put people before profits, and family values that fully fund opportunities for low-income families. If, as a society, we truly value equal opportunity for all, then we cannot claim there is a fair race being run, when some people are not even at the starting line. Call it restitution, or a chance to catch up—or simply call it justice.

5

Women Face Discrimination in the Workplace

Julie Lowell

Julie Lowell is an intern for United for a Fair Economy, a non-profit organization that opposes the concentration of wealth and economic power in the hands of a small group of Americans.

Despite the best efforts of the women's rights movement, women continue to earn substantially less money than men. This has resulted in an unequal society in which working women are poorer, unhealthier, and less secure in retirement than their male counterparts. Although women perform some of the most important jobs in society as nurses, caregivers, and teachers they are expected to live lives of financial hardship. Parity in pay is the only way to alleviate this problem. Otherwise there will never be gender equality in the workforce.

In the 1970s, the Women's Rights movement demanded equality, pressing for equal opportunity to the workplace, access to all occupations, to equal pay not just for equal work, but for comparable work. Alongside the Civil Rights movement, women pushed for economic security for all.

And we have come a long way. Women have gained greater access to formal education, and increased labor market participation. A union movement dominated by SEIU [Service Employees International Union] and UNITE HERE [Union of

Needletrades Industrial, Textile and Hotel Employees and Restaurant Employees] are increasingly involved in organizing occupations that are primarily filled with women, with the majority of their members now being women. The Equal Pay Act of 1963 and the Civil Rights Act of 1964 have also contributed to a rise in wages, and a lessening of the gap between male and female workers. In 1960, women earned 59 cents for every dollar that men earned. By 2002, this gap lessened by 18 cents, as women made 77 cents for every dollar that men earned. In fact, the policy victories benefited women more than African Americans, who still make only 57 cents on the white man's dollar.

Gender equity does not yet exist in the US.

Where We Are Now

But we must be careful not to let such gains for women lull us into a false sense of security and hopefulness. Gender equity does not yet exist in the U.S. Women's median annual income today is $30,100, a number that is approximately three-quarters of the median annual income of men. Based on past rates of wage growth, women's wages will not reach parity with men's until at least 2051. Equality will take even longer when taking race into account. It is also important to note that the gap between men's and women's wages has been closing partially due to an increase in women's wages but also due to a decrease in men's wages. One of the consequences of this has been that living wages are increasingly rare, forcing both parents to work, and adding an increased burden on women as they are expected to continue the caregiver role in addition to being in the workplace.

In 2002, the Department of Labor reported that women compose 46% of the US workforce, and are found in disproportionately lower paying jobs than men. While women make up a larger percentage of college graduates than men today, women are more likely to major in medical professions such as nursing and care work (18 percent vs. 6 percent), and education (10 percent vs. 4 percent), while men are more likely to major in business and management (26 percent vs. 19 percent), and engineering (12 percent vs. 2 percent). The degrees held at a higher rate by men often correlate with higher salaries.

In order to fully capture the picture of racial inequality, it is most telling to compare women's wages to white men's wages. This calculation excludes wages received by men of color, wages that are considerably lower than white men's, hence if included they would considerably bring down the median men's wage. The Institute for Women's Policy Research (IWPR), found that women's median annual earnings were 67.5% that of white men's. When broken down by race, white women make 70.0% of what white men make, Asian American women 75.0%, African American women 62.5%, Hispanic women 52.5%, and Native American women 57.8%.

Even these numbers need refining to get the real picture. From this information it appears that Asian American women are doing very well, but when looking more specifically at Asian American ethnicities, it is shown that Japanese Americans are most likely to earn the highest wages as $250/hour, while Vietnamese Americans are likely to earn the lowest at $5/hour.

Why the Gap Continues

Some may argue that this gap is based on differences between men and women in "human capital", or work skills that have been acquired. This argument claims that men's higher levels of education, job force training, and/ or work experience account for them holding higher paying jobs in comparison to women. However, a study by the US General Accounting Of fice in 2003 found that only 55% of the Gender Wage Gap is determined by differences in human capital, industry and occupation, unionization, and work hours.

Among the highest earning, high level executives in Fortune 500 companies, only 5.2% were women.

It is also important to ask what creates varying levels of human capital acquisition—i.e. educational attainment, job training and work experience. Is some of this variety a result of gender discrimination? Due to different biological roles of men and women, are woman penalized in the job market, denied the same training and advancements? Women are certainly underrepresented in higher paying jobs. As cited by the IWPR report, in 2002, a Catalyst study found that among the highest earning, high level executives in Fortune 500 companies, only 5.2% were women.

Finally, one of the most important questions to ask is why are there such differing compensation rates based on different working roles in society? Jobs that have been viewed as "women's work," such as care giving and cleaning, are still predominantly filled by women, especially women of color, and are consistently paid less than a living wage. These are jobs that are some of the most important and most challenging in our society.

One prime example is the position of home health aides. The US Department of Labor's Bureau of Labor Statistics characterizes this job as having high physical and emotional demands, yet modest entry requirements, low pay, and lack of advancement opportunities. These high physical and emotional demands include assisting patients with eating, dressing, bathing, and medicating, while at times being the only person of contact for that day or week. Home health aides also have the responsibility of cleaning waste. Risks of the job include back injuries, minor infections, contracting major diseases, and assault from disoriented or mentally ill patients.

Women who are financially insecure live more stressful, frenzied day-to-day lives, have decreased quality of health and are unable to exercise choices.

In 2002, the median salary for home health aides was $8.70 per hour, with the lowest 10 percent of workers earning less than $6.76 per hour. Generally this does not include travel time. In 2004, there were 2,921,000 nursing, psychiatric and home health aides combined, women comprising 89.3 percent of this workforce, African Americans comprising 25.9 percent of aides, and Hispanic and Latinos making up 13.1 percent of aides. This is in comparison to women making up 46.5 percent of the general work force, African Americans making up 10.7 percent and Hispanic and Latinos comprising 12.9 percent. . . . Who among us would say that care for our aging parents is worth so little? What income would many men give up if there were no women to do this work?

Long-Term Implications

What are the long-term implications of such disparity? It ultimately comes down to a lack of financial security, especially for single, working mothers. Women who are financially insecure live more stressful, frenzied day-to-day lives, have decreased quality of health and are unable to exercise choices. In 2002, 12.1 percent of single women were in poverty, while only 8.7 percent of men were in poverty. In looking specifically at single moms, 28.9 percent are in poverty, while married couples with children only have a poverty rate of 7.1 percent. By race, single mother poverty rates are 22.1 percent for white women, 22.4 percent for Asian American women, 35.4 percent for black women, 36.3 percent for Hispanic women, and 37.8 percent for Native American women. In addition to the difficulties of day-to-day life based on such low income, this lack of financial security also continues into retirement.

A report entitled "Gender and Economic Security," published by the Institute for Women's Policy Research used data from the 1999–2001 Current Population Surveys to better understand economic security in retirement. This report found that 90 percent of the population 65 and older receives Social Security, with women receiving a median benefit of $7750, in 2002 adjusted currency, while men receive a median benefit of $11,040. In addition, 60 percent of women receive income from assets (interest, dividends, and rent), while 65 percent of men have income via assets. However, for women the median annual benefit is $1330 while it is $1650 for men. Only 37 percent of women receive pension benefits, with a median annual benefit of $5600. 47 percent of men receive pension benefits, with a median annual benefit of $10,340. Another source of income for seniors is employment. 12 percent of women and 22 percent of men continue to have earnings. For these women, their median annual income is 60 percent of men's.

Women's Social Security compensation, pension compensations and other sources of income in retirement are strikingly different in comparison to men's as a result of women's lower lifetime earnings. This is due to women working less in the paid economy in order to take on the caregiver role, women being paid disproportionately less than men for the work they do, and women composing a larger portion of lower paying fields. This economic burden in retirement falls even more heavily on single women who have never been married and on divorced women, as they do not have the option of eventually receiving widow's compensation, which is the entirety of one's husband's social security dividends. The economic burden is further stretched due to the fact that women live longer than men. Ultimately, this means a lower quality of living and a challenged daily existence for women throughout their working years and into retirement.

Unfinished Business

This article highlights those women who have no choice but to continue working difficult, unsafe jobs for too little compensation. However, many of today's inequalities are less obvious, meaning that they could become more insidious if complacency sets in. For example, the privatization of Social Security could potentially mean less financial stability for senior citizens, leading to an increased need for uncompensated care. If this is the case, it is most likely that women, such as daughters or wives, will be picking up this duty, while still working in the workplace and at home. This double and triple burden is not acceptable. We must advocate for and support policy initiatives that increase access to higher education, that call for a living wage, and we must continue to challenge mainstream perceptions that the social value of the work of caring for others must be matched with a commensurate financial value.

The women's movement has experienced a lot of success, but now is the time that a concerted effort has to be made to keep pushing boundaries to parity. As in the 1960's, to accomplish our ends, a strong alliance with communities of color needs to be cemented. Women of color are at the intersection of both constituencies; if their voices are heard and their needs are met, our work towards equality will be closer to being done.

6

Women Do Not Face Discrimination in the Workplace

Diana Furchtgott-Roth

Diana Furchtgott-Roth is the coauthor of Women's Figures: The Economic Progress of Women in America *and a senior fellow and director of the Center for Employment Policy at the Hudson Institute. From 2003 to 2005 she served as chief economist at the U.S. Department of Labor.*

Many members of the women's movement claim that a so-called glass ceiling prevents women from moving into executive positions in corporations. While the term has been widely used in the press, there is no such thing as a glass ceiling. The reason there are fewer women CEOs has to do with choices made by women themselves. Most women prefer to play a greater role in raising their children than their male partners and therefore do not choose to work the long hours and many years that are required for promotion to the executive suites. Those who choose to make such sacrifices can and do achieve executive status, and women today are represented in the highest levels of government and business. Accusations of gender inequality are a disservice to women who have achieved parity with men through dedication to hard work. Until a majority of women decide to work sixty hours a week in order to climb the ladder of success, they should not expect to earn the same salaries and positions as those who do make that commitment.

It has become fashionable to talk about a glass ceiling for women, an invisible career barrier which cannot be overcome by hardworking females with even the most impeccable qualifications. It's a sad story of women who work shoulder to shoulder with men and then, just as that chief executive officer job comes into view presto!, the glass barrier descends. The men move up; the women are left behind.

The glass ceiling was given the seal of credibility with the federal Glass Ceiling Commission in 1991, which put out a ponderous report authenticating these claims. And other institutions periodically release studies showing that women make up only a small fraction of corporate officers at the nation's largest companies. The conclusion of all these studies, of course, is that life is unfair to women, who need special affirmative-action programs to progress in the workplace.

But is this sad story true, or is it just the fantasy of a group of whiny females for whom the tale of the glass ceiling is a convenient way of advancing their own interests? In fact, the glass ceiling is a figment of feminist imaginations, up there with the myths of Alar poisoning [in apples], and Jews eating Christian babies on Passover.

Women Portrayed as Victims

Why was this tale concocted? The answer is obvious: It's in the interests of feminists to portray women as victims, since it gives women greater economic benefits. Who wouldn't want preferred access to government contracts, promotion of less-qualified members of their group over others and a whole apparatus set up to ensure proper representation of their relevant group? As a woman professional, I should be delighted, except that it imposes substantial economic costs on society as a whole, shared by all consumers and taxpayers.

Efforts in corporations, universities and governments to counteract the so-called glass ceiling in the name of equality rely on a whole cadre of "diversity specialists" whose role is to

ensure equal representation of various groups in different professions. Corporations hold sensitivity training rather than computer training and promote the less-qualified to managerial positions to be "fair." Universities have quotas for female faculty and governments have minority set-asides.

All of this costs money, reduces efficiency and results in higher prices for corporations' products, higher tuition costs at universities and higher taxes for individuals. Economic growth is slowed, reducing job creation—the most important avenue for everyone's advancement. Yes, some women win—but everyone else pays for it.

Since 1982 women have earned more than 50 percent of all bachelor's degrees and all master's degrees, and in other fields women are closing the gap fast.

Substantial Improvements

Just consider some facts: Today women are well-represented in the professions; they continue to enter fields of study previously dominated by men; they are starting their own businesses in record numbers; and they are winning elective office throughout the country. Laws barring discrimination against women are on the books and enforced. All those gains clearly contradict the image of women as victims struggling against discrimination in the workplace.

Since 1982 women have earned more than 50 percent of all bachelor's degrees and all master's degrees, and in other fields women are closing the gap fast. Whereas 2 or 3 percent of all law degrees awarded went to women in the fifties and sixties and 5 percent in 1970, women [in 2005] . . . earn about 43 percent of those degrees. Fewer than 1 percent of dentistry degrees were awarded to women in the fifties, sixties and seventies, yet women now receive 38 percent of these degrees. Similar trends hold for doctoral and medical degrees. In 1996

women represented 54 percent of the class admitted to Yale Medical School. As they move into previously male-dominated fields, women's wages have been steadily rising relative to men's wages. It is true that, on average, women earn less than men, when all women's wages are averaged with all men's wages. But that is because these averages compare people who have different educational backgrounds and who have chosen different jobs and different hours. When comparing wages, like should be compared to like, not nurses to engineers.

Among people ages 27 to 33 who never have had a child, women's earnings are close to 98 percent of men's.

In studies accounting for demographic and job characteristics such as education, race, age, part- or full-time employment, public- or private-sector status, occupation and union or nonunion status, women earn almost as much as men. The National Longitudinal Survey of Youth found that, among people ages 27 to 33 who never have had a child, women's earnings are close to 98 percent of men's. A study of economics and engineering doctorates by June O'Neill came up with similar results. However, many women choose occupations and careers that allow them more flexibility in work hours, and these positions typically pay less.

Gains in the Business World

Furthermore, the wage gap widens once women have children, presumably since the children place additional demands on these women's time.

The most outstanding gains made by women lately have been in the business world. In 1972 there were only 400,000 women-owned businesses. Today there are approximately 8 million such businesses in the United States, employing 15.5 million people and generating $1.4 trillion in sales. The number of women-owned businesses increased 43 percent from 1987 to 1992. Women are starting businesses at twice the rate of men.

With all this progress, why did the Glass Ceiling Commission conclude that only 5 percent of senior managers at Fortune 2000 companies are women, leading to charges of glass ceilings and discrimination? Because the commission used a statistically corrupt methodology to prove its point and further its agenda. Rather than comparing the number of women qualified to hold top positions with those who actually hold those jobs, it compared the number of women in the labor force, without reference to experience or education levels, with those wielding power at top corporations. This resulted in a politically useful low number of 5 percent.

Moving in and out of the workforce in accordance with family demands is not conducive to being a CEO of a major corporation.

Sixty-Hour Work Weeks

The real answer is that there are comparatively few educated and experienced women available to be nominated for such high level positions. Typical qualifications for top management positions include both a master's degree in business administration and 25 years of work experience, and there aren't many such women around. Look at the data: Women received less than 5 percent of graduate degrees in the sixties and seventies, and these are the graduates who now are at the pinnacle of their professions. That supports the "pipeline" theory, which holds that women have not reached the top in greater numbers because they have not been "in the pipeline" long enough.

Moreover, to reach the CEO level, individuals have to be committed to their jobs and work 60-hour weeks continuously throughout their career. Many men and many women, especially mothers, do not want to do this. Moving in and out of the work force in accordance with family demands is not conducive to being a CEO of a major corporation. Yet many mothers do interrupt their careers in just this fashion, since these mothers believe that they are the best caregivers for their children.

There is nothing wrong with choosing a career which allows more time at home with less pay rather than one with more time at work with more pay, and in either case women should not be considered victims of a glass ceiling and in need of government intervention such as affirmative action. One consequence of those choices, however, is that out of the relatively small group of women who have the educational requirements and training to be CEOs—those who got their graduate degrees in the sixties—fewer have put in the 25 years of 60-hour weeks that a CEO position requires. The result is a small pool of qualified women for those kinds of positions.

The good news is that in the future more women will be getting the necessary educational qualifications and more of those who graduated in the seventies and later will be moving into corporate positions, so the trend toward increasing numbers of female corporate executives will continue. However, because of the unique position that mothers play in rearing children, the ratio of male to female CEOs is unlikely to reach 50–50. This is not necessarily bad. The important point is that women should be free to choose their career paths.

The Glass Ceiling Is a Myth

Now, if outcomes at the CEO level are not likely to be 50–50 on their own, does that show that women face a glass ceiling? Not at all: The data make it clear that women now have equality of opportunity and that those who choose to rise to high positions in corporations can do so. Cultural barriers to women in top positions largely have disappeared—just ask [former] Secretary of State Madeleine Albright. When discrimination does occur, there are legal remedies to deal with it under the Civil Rights Act and the Equal Pay Act. Women are bringing these cases to court and winning.

Whereas the glass-ceiling myth benefits women in the short run, its effects well could backfire against women over the long term. With special preferences for women in the workplace, the achievements of all women can be called into question, since it can be assumed that progress has been made because of quotas and preferences rather than ability. When Albright's selection was announced, there was some speculation that President Clinton had chosen her because of her sex rather than because of her preeminent qualifications. Albright was confirmed by the Senate irrespective of these doubts. But the patients shopping for heart surgeons or the retirees looking for financial planners well may prefer to put their lives and their money into male hands, even though the particular female heart surgeons and financial planners under consideration may not have benefited from affirmative action.

Some say that women in America face a glass ceiling: that they are paid less than men; that they cannot reach the highest rungs of the corporate ladder; that they cannot enter any profession they choose; that they would benefit from more government intervention in the marketplace; and that they need affirmative action and quotas. But none of these is true. These views are being advanced because it is in feminists' interests for women to have preferential treatment and to have all consumers and taxpayers pay for it. It's a great scam—and they're getting away with it.

7

Gay Couples
Have Equal Rights

Ilana Mercer

Ilana Mercer is an analyst and blogger for the Free-Market News Network and the author of Broad Sides: One Woman's Clash with a Corrupt Culture.

According to the libertarian definition of rights, Americans have the basic rights of life, liberty, and property. Marriage, however, is not a right. In fact, marriage is not mentioned in the Constitution, and the government should not be involved in sanctioning marriages at all. It therefore follows that not allowing homosexual couples to participate in state-sanctioned marriage does not violate their basic rights and does not constitute inequality under the law. Gay couples who want to solemnize their commitment may do so through private vows, living wills, and other contracts. Beyond Social Security benefits, married couples do not have many benefits that gay couples cannot obtain by making private contracts.

It might be news to the noisome Mayor [Gavin] Newsome of San Francisco, but it should not be news to libertarians: Not conferring the benefits of marriage on homosexual unions does *not* in the least violate the rights of gays. Not if we adhere to the libertarian definition of rights as the inalienable rights to life, liberty and property. Since these are the only rights libertarians wish the state to enforce, equality under the law is thus the requirement that the state not deprive any person of life, liberty, or property, without due process.

Having one's relationship blessed by the state simply does not constitute a basic right.

Having one's relationship blessed by the state simply does not constitute a basic right.

To suggest this is the case is to equate state-granted *benefits* with *rights*, and *different* treatment with *discrimination*. To claim gays are denied basic rights is to base one's claim on a monumental misconstruing of the concept of individual rights.

Furthermore, a linguistic definition is not a semantic flight of fancy, but a description of the nature of a thing. The ever-so-mod New Oxford American Dictionary defines marriage as "the formal union of a man and a woman." Based on the inherent qualities of the thing being described, "marriage" is clearly different from "same-sex unions." Setting aside the view some egalitarians hold that this definition must be made more inclusive, why is it irrational or unfair for the state to treat a thing in accordance with its properties or nature?

Notwithstanding that libertarians do not approve of state benefits, for the state to allot different—or no—benefits to different entities does not amount to unequal treatment under the law. If it did, an employed person could demand the "right" to claim welfare benefits while employed.

Treating gay couples ... differently than married people isn't inequality under the law, because their rights to life, liberty and property are not denied.

Egalitarians, however, do not like the fact that reality-based, objective dissimilarities, give rise to disparate treatment. They thus resort to inflammatory civil-rights rhetoric. However, it doesn't change the fact that treating gay couples (or heterosexual cohabitants, for that matter) differently than married people isn't inequality under the law, because their rights to life, liberty and property are not denied.

Civil Rights Tyranny

More proof that gay couples' rights are not being infringed is the fact that nothing prevents them from solemnizing their commitments through promises, vows, contracts and living wills. Other than the Social Security provision, which ought to be privatized, there aren't really many so-called benefits the state confers on married couples that are not available to gays through private contracts.

The rousing raves about discrimination aside, if we define rights properly, we must conclude that gay couples are not being denied their *individual rights*.

Ideally, government should be entirely divorced from the nuptial business. But from the fact that the state upholds traditional marriage, why does it follow that it is violating the individual rights of same-sex couples who clearly don't fit the definition or the profile?

Changing the definition of marriage to include gay unions will inevitably broaden the scope of the civil-rights tyranny. If the history of the civil-rights revolution is anything to go by, creating new categories to protect and to privilege is bound to extend the legal reach of these couples (and their lawyers) to pockets and property not their own, in essence leading to more violations of the rights of employers, landlords and . . . perhaps parents. If [gay marriages were legalized] fathers (and, presumably, mothers) will have to share visitation rights or even custody with the lesbian (or homosexual) partner of their child's biological parent.

An expansion of this kind in government power is indubitably undesirable.

Privatize Marriage

Ideally, religious institutions ought to act as the ministers of marriage. If marriage were thus privatized, *conservatives* would have to accept that some liberal churches and synagogues (the mullahs in their mosques would resist) will wed homosexuals.

If federalism were respected, *liberals* and leftist *libertarians* would equally have to live with the fact that the people of most states would probably not extend to other unions the protections they afford marriage—38 states have so far passed laws, the implication of which is to confine marriage benefits to those who fall within the known definition.

Like it or not, the American scheme, and the (now sadly obsolete) 10th Amendment, dictates that whatever is not specified as a power of the federal government and is not prohibited to the states, is reserved to the states or the people.

This applies to the sanctimonious Mayor Newsome whose campy coup—issuing marriage licenses to same-sex couples in contravention of state law—did not rest on any coherent notion of individual rights. It sprung, rather, from the invented, casuistic constitutional doctrine that arose in the wake of the illegally ratified 14th Amendment [that guarantees equal protection under the law].

The mayor should meditate on the meaning of one of the most magnificent documents of political philosophy, which states that, "Governments are instituted among Men, deriving their just Powers from the Consent of the Governed."

8

Gay Couples Do Not Have Equal Rights

Evan Wolfson

Evan Wolfson is a lawyer who has argued for gay rights before the Supreme Court and is the executive director of Freedom to Marry, an organization working to make gay marriage legal. In 2004 he was named by Time *magazine as one of the one hundred most influential people in the world.*

Marriage is more than a loving bond between two people—it also provides more than a thousand legal benefits to married couples. Because gay couples are prevented from marrying in forty-eight states, most gay partners cannot participate in a full range of critical legal matters concerning housing, insurance, retirement, taxes, parenting, and even death. Rights that heterosexual couples take for granted, such as making emergency medical decisions for a spouse, are often denied to homosexual couples. The prerogative to make such life and death decisions should not be seen as a special privilege for gays but as a basic right for all. The United States must end its institutional prejudice against gay people and allow them to marry so they can enjoy all the legal rights guaranteed to heterosexual couples.

Depending on which linguistic expert you ask, there are anywhere from two thousand to seven thousand different languages spoken in the world today. That's a huge number to put your mind around—even for someone who lives in Manhattan, where seemingly hundreds of those languages can be heard on the subway on any given day. Still, I'm willing to bet that each of these languages has something in common with the others: a word that means marriage.

No matter what language people speak—from Arabic to Yiddish, from Chinook to Chinese—marriage is what we use to describe a specific relationship of love and dedication to another person. It is how we explain the families that are united because of that love. And it universally signifies a level of self-sacrifice and responsibility and a stage of life unlike any other.

Now of course, different cultures and times have had many different conceptions of marriage, different rules and different ways of regarding those who are married—not to mention different treatment for married men and married women. . . .

But with all this variety and all the changes that have occurred in marriage over time and in different places, including our country and within our lifetime, it is clear that marriage has been a defining institution in virtually every society throughout history. Given its variety and omnipresence, it is not surprising that when people talk about marriage, they often mean different things.

Consider all the different dimensions of marriage in the United States alone. First, marriage is a personal commitment and an important choice that belongs to couples in love. In fact, many people consider their choice of partner the most significant choice they will ever make. It is a relationship between people who are, hopefully, in love and an undertaking that most couples hope will endure.

Marriage is also a social statement, preeminently describing and defining a person's relationships and place in society. Marital status, along with what we do for a living, is often one of the first pieces of information we give to others about ourselves. It's so important, in fact, that most married people wear a symbol of their marriage on their hand.

The federal government cataloged more than 1,049 ways in which married people are accorded special status under federal law.

Marriage is also a relationship between a couple and the government. Couples need the government's participation to get into and out of a marriage. Because it is a legal or "civil" institution, marriage is the legal gateway to a vast array of protections, responsibilities, and benefits—most of which cannot be replicated in any other way, no matter how much forethought you show or how much you are able to spend on attorneys' fees and assembling proxies and papers.

A Major Safety Net

The tangible legal and economic protections and responsibilities that come with marriage include access to health care and medical decision making for your partner and your children; parenting and immigration rights; inheritance, taxation, Social Security, and other government benefits; rules for ending a relationship while protecting both parties; and the simple ability to pool resources to buy or transfer property without adverse tax treatment. In 1996, the federal government cataloged more than 1,049 ways in which married people are accorded special status under federal law; in a 2004 report, the General Accounting Office bumped up those federal effects of marriage to at least 1,138. Add in the state-level protections and the intangible as well as tangible privileges marriage brings in private life, and it's clear that the legal institution of marriage is one of the major safety nets in life, both in times of crisis and in day-to-day living. . . .

Skirmishes and Changes

[Marriage] has historically been a battlefield, the site of collisions within and between governments and religions over who should regulate it. But marriage has weathered centuries of skirmishes and change. It has evolved from an institution that was imposed on some people and denied to others, to the loving union of companionship, commitment, and caring between equal partners that we think of today. . . .

Americans have been ready again and again to make the changes needed to ensure that the institution of marriage reflects the values of love, inclusion, interdependence, and support.

But fortunately, the general story of our country is movement toward inclusion and equality. The majority of Americans are fair. They realize that exclusionary conceptions of marriage fly in the face of our national commitment to freedom as well as the personal commitment made by loving couples. Americans have been ready again and again to make the changes needed to ensure that the institution of marriage reflects the values of love, inclusion, interdependence, and support.

Such a change came about as recently as 1987, when a group of Americans who had been denied the freedom to marry came before the U.S. Supreme Court. Before the justices issued an opinion in the case, *Turner v. Safley*, they had to determine what role marriage plays in American society. Or, more precisely, what role marriage plays in American law.

After careful consideration, the justices outlined four "important attributes" of marriage: First, they said, marriage represents an opportunity to make a public statement of commitment and love to another person, and an opportunity to receive public support for that commitment. Second, the justices said, marriage has for many people an important spiritual or religious dimension. Third, marriage offers the prospect of physical "consummation," which of course most of us call something else. And fourth, the justices said, marriage in the United States is the unique and indispensable gateway, the "precondition," for a vast array of protections, responsibilities, and benefits—public and private, tangible and intangible, legal and economic—that have real importance for real people.

The Supreme Court of course understood, as we discussed above, that marriage has other purposes and aspects in the religious sphere, in business, and in people's personal lives. The justices knew, for example, that for many people, marriage is also important as a structure in which they can have and raise children. But when examined with the U.S. Constitution in mind, these four attributes or interests identified by the Court are the ones that have the legal weight. And after weighing these attributes, the justices ruled—in a unanimous decision—that marriage is such an important choice that it may not be arbitrarily denied by the government. Accordingly, they ordered that the government stop refusing marriage licenses to the group of Americans who had brought the case.

That group of Americans was prisoners.

Unlike spouses, unmarried partners are usually not considered next of kin for the purposes of hospital visitation and emergency medical decisions.

Seventeen years after the Supreme Court recognized that the choice to marry is so important that it cannot be arbitrarily denied to convicted felons, one group of Americans is still denied the freedom to marry. No matter how long they have been together as a couple, no matter how committed and loving their relationship, and no matter how much they need the basic tools and support that come with marriage, lesbian and gay Americans in [most states in] this country are excluded from the legal right to obtain a civil marriage license and marry the person they love. . . .

Unfair Treatment of Gay Couples

Exclusion from the freedom to marry unfairly punishes committed same-sex couples and their families by depriving them of critical assistance, security, and obligations in virtually every area of life, including, yes, even death and taxes:

- Death: If a couple is not married and one partner dies, the other partner is not entitled to get bereavement leave from work, to file wrongful death claims, to draw the Social Security payments of the deceased partner, or to automatically inherit a shared home, assets, or personal items in the absence of a will.

- Debts: Unmarried partners do not generally have responsibility for each other's debt.

- Divorce: Unmarried couples do not have access to the courts or to the legal and financial guidelines in times of breakup, including rules for how to handle shared property, child support, and alimony, or to protect the weaker party and the kids.

- Family leave: Unmarried couples are often not covered by laws and policies that permit people to take medical leave to care for a sick spouse or for the kids.

- Health: Unlike spouses, unmarried partners are usually not considered next of kin for the purposes of hospital visitation and emergency medical decisions. In addition, they can't cover their families on their health plans without paying taxes on the coverage, nor are they eligible for Medicare and Medicaid coverage.

- Housing: Denied marriage, couples of lesser means are not recognized as a family and thus can be denied or disfavored in their applications for public housing.

- Immigration: U.S. residency and family unification are not available to an unmarried partner from another country.

- Inheritance: Unmarried surviving partners do not automatically inherit property should their loved one die without a will, nor do they get legal protection for inheritance rights such as elective share or to bypass the hassles and expenses of probate court.

- Insurance: Unmarried partners can't always sign up for joint home and auto insurance. In addition, many employers don't cover domestic partners or their biological or nonbiological children in their health insurance plans.

- Parenting: Unmarried couples are denied the automatic right to joint parenting, joint adoption, joint foster care, and visitation for nonbiological parents. In addition, the children of unmarried couples are denied the guarantee of child support and an automatic legal relationship to both parents, and are sometimes sent a wrongheaded but real negative message about their own status and family.

- Portability: Unlike marriages, which are honored in all states and countries, domestic partnerships and other alternative mechanisms only exist in a few states and countries, are not given any legal acknowledgment in most, and leave families without the clarity and security of knowing what their legal status and rights will be.

- Privilege: Unmarried couples are not shielded against having to testify against each other in judicial proceedings, and are also usually denied the coverage in crime-victims counseling and protection programs afforded married couples.

- Property: Unmarried couples are excluded from special rules that permit married couples to buy and own property together under favorable terms, rules that protect married couples in their shared homes, and rules regarding the distribution of property in the event of death or divorce.

- Retirement: In addition to being denied access to shared or spousal benefits through Social Security as well as coverage under Medicare and other programs, unmarried couples are denied withdrawal rights and protective tax treatment given to spouses with regard to IRAs and other retirement plans.

- Taxes: Unmarried couples cannot file joint tax returns and are excluded from tax benefits and claims specific to marriage. In addition, they are denied the right to transfer property to each other and pool the family's resources without adverse tax consequences.

And, again, virtually all of these critical, concrete legal incidents of marriage cannot be arranged by shelling out money for an attorney or writing up private agreements, even if the couple has lots of forethought to discuss all the issues in advance and then a bunch of extra cash to throw at lawyers. . . .

The Freedom to Marry

I'm not using terms like "gay marriage" or "same-sex marriage." That's because these terms imply that same-sex couples are asking for rights and privileges that married couples do not have, or for rights that are something lesser or different than what non-gay couples have. In fact, we don't want "gay marriage," we want marriage—the same freedom to marry, with the same duties, dignity, security, and expression of love and equality as our non-gay brothers and sisters have.

Gay people have the same mix of reasons for wanting the freedom to marry as non-gay people; emotional and economic, practical and personal, social and spiritual.

Gay people have the same mix of reasons for wanting the freedom to marry as non-gay people: emotional and economic, practical and personal, social and spiritual. The inequities and the legal and cultural second-class status that exclusion from marriage reinforces affect all gay people, but the denial of marriage's safety net falls hardest on the poor, the less educated, and the otherwise vulnerable. And the denial of the freedom to marry undermines young gay people's sense of self and their dreams of a life together with a partner.

Of course our country needs to find ways other than marriage to support and welcome all kids, all families, and all communities. Marriage is not, need not, and should not be the only means of protecting oneself and a loving partner or family. But like other Americans, same-sex couples need the responsibilities and support marriage offers legally and economically to families dealing with parenting, property, Social Security, finances, and the like, especially in times of crisis, health emergency, divorce, and death. And gay people, like all human beings, love and want to declare love, want inclusion in the community and the equal choices and possibilities that belong to us all as Americans.

Marriage equality is the precondition for these rights, these protections, this inclusion, this full citizenship. The freedom to marry is important in building strong families and strong communities. What sense does it make to deny that freedom to [gay couples]? . . .

How many more young people have to grow up believing that they are alone, that they are not welcome, that they are unequal and second-class, that their society does not value their love or expect them to find permanence and commitment?

How many non-gay parents and family members have to worry or feel pain for their gay loved ones? What mother doesn't want the best for all her kids, or want to be able to dance at her lesbian daughter's wedding just as she did at her other child's?

As Americans have done so many times in the past, it's time we learn from our mistakes and acknowledge that lesbian and gay Americans—like people the world around—speak the vocabulary of marriage, live the personal commitment of marriage, do the hard work of marriage, and share the responsibilities we associate with marriage. It's time to allow them the same freedom every other American has—the freedom to marry.

9

The Health Care System Is Racist

Sally Lehrman

Sally Lehrman is an award-winning independent journalist who covers health policy, health care, and medical technology for national consumer magazines, newsletters, and media including Nature, Scientific American, Health, Ms., Salon.com, *and the* Washington Post.

Health care statistics show a pattern of racism and discrimination. Blacks, Hispanics, and Native Americans receive lower quality health care than white Americans, which leads to a greater likelihood of disease and premature death for these minorities. Various studies reveal that doctors are less likely to give minorities the aggressive treatment that is needed to fight serious diseases including cancer. The racial health divide has created an unequal society where a person's overall health may be determined by the color of his or her skin. Unless this disparity is remedied, society will suffer.

Hoping to find out why adult-onset diabetes strikes Native Americans three times as often as whites, government researchers are narrowing in on a gene prevalent in Pima Indians. Concerned about the high rate among African Americans, Howard University scientists are collecting DNA samples from West Africans with the disease.

But the push to find genetic differences and develop targeted medicines won't ease sharp disparities in health status

Sally Lehrman, "Race and Healthcare,"*Alternet*, October 1, 2003. Reproduced by permission of the author.

between whites and other racial groups in the United States, insist some social scientists and health specialists. While acknowledging that biology may be an important contributor to disease susceptibility and severity, they say social factors are key to bridging the gap. Dozens of genes may be involved in diabetes, for example, but they act in concert with our ability to get exercise, find healthy food and see a sympathetic doctor for the medical care we need. They say racism—not race—is what makes people of color more sick.

Racism—not race—is what makes people of color more sick.

"There is undue emphasis on genetics at the expense of societal factors," says Barbara Koenig, a Stanford University anthropologist who studies contemporary biomedicine. "If you look at the history of improvements in life expectancy in the industrialized West, the things that made the most difference in terms of overall health status were not medical interventions, but those in the social domain."

Social stratification, residential segregation and neglect all contribute to the higher rates of disease and death among U.S. ethnic and racial minorities, says Carmen Nevarez, medical director of the Public Health Institute in Oakland, California. The roots of obesity—and diabetes—are easy to see among her own young, urban clients, she points out. Without a nearby grocery store, these teenagers have few options other than a bag of Cheetos for a cheap, easy breakfast. They have no structured exercise in school, and are afraid to walk outdoors for fear of being arrested or caught in gang crossfire.

Racial Health Divide

But the most critical social factor may be the health care system itself, conclude medical and public health experts at the Institute of Medicine. In a comprehensive analysis of 100 studies on treatment and outcome differences by race, they conclude that biological differences in susceptibility and disease severity aren't enough to explain the racial health divide. Instead, their recent book-length report, "Unequal Treatment: Confronting Racial and Ethnic Disparities in Healthcare," blames a pattern of lower-quality service stemming from cost-containment pressures, clinical bureaucracy, inconveniently located hospitals, and other factors, including unconscious biases held by doctors.

In one comprehensive study of 1.7 million patients, African Americans received major therapeutic procedures less often than whites in 37 of 77 conditions.

"Even with the same symptoms and stage of the disease, differences persist," says Brian Smedley, project director for the study, which also controls for insurance coverage and ability to pay. The committee found stark inequalities in preventive care, diagnostics and treatment no matter what the disease, and these in turn connected to higher rates of mortality. Blacks and Latinos who arrived at hospitals with the same severity of heart disease, for example, received catheterization or bypass surgery less often. African Americans with a colorectal tumor were 41 percent less likely than whites to receive major treatment such as cutting out the cancerous cells.

In one comprehensive study of 1.7 million patients, African Americans received major therapeutic procedures less often than whites in 37 of 77 conditions, according to the report. In contrast, minority patients underwent limb amputations in greater proportions and were given antipsychotic medications more often. "Clearly, these disparities are unacceptable and they require a comprehensive response to correct them," Smedley says.

A Call for Data

The report recommended structural changes in health services delivery, such as strengthening long-term relationships between doctors and patients, providing clear guidelines for care, and offering training in cultural competence. It also underlined what the authors saw as a critical need for consistent data on patient and provider race, ethnicity, and language, as well as ways these might affect the process, structure, and outcomes of care.

"The federal dataset is very limited," says Smedley. Indeed, a 2001 Commonwealth Fund report found that health agencies' efforts to collect statistics by race, ethnicity and language were sorely lacking, despite widespread agreement on their value in improving care quality and access....

Some have proposed that racial categories themselves can contribute to unequal health status. Even the Institute of Medicine committee acknowledged that skin color, racial identity and ancestry don't always match up. Focusing on race in medicine can reinforce misperceptions that it represents biological reality instead of a social ideology, the health specialists said. More dangerously, argues sociologist Yehudi Webster at California State University–Los Angeles in the American Sociological Association newsletter, race classifications can trigger the very attitudes and awareness that may underlie differential care by doctors.

Racial Factors Need to Be Studied

Similarly, scientists' enthusiasm about pinpointing biological and cultural reasons for health disparities can bolster popular racist stereotypes and hierarchies, anthropologist Koenig says. "If we focus on individual (genetic) variation in particular populations, we almost always get into a 'blame the victim' mentality," she says. Groups more often affected by a disease can become stigmatized, Koenig explained, especially if the condition involves risk factors connected to lifestyle. Anti-gay activists, for example, have fixated on HIV's connection to sexual activity that they regard as immoral.

But that doesn't mean "race" is not a useful tool to understand health disparities, according to Koenig. Even as geneticists debate the biological relevance of race, agreement is broad that its social categories deeply influence well-being. Sometimes the cause is quite direct, as when darker skin among African Americans correlates with more experiences of prejudice—and not coincidentally, researchers conclude, higher rates of hypertension.

A Legacy of Poor Access

The Institute of Medicine details a sharpening disparity in care beginning with the closing of black hospitals in the 1960s. Minority communities lost convenient geographic access and a sense of familiarity and safety, while African American doctors found themselves shut out. "What's surprising is this gap hasn't closed," says study leader Smedley. "We would expect this 40 years ago because of discrimination, gross disparities between economic status, and lack of insurance."

Cost-containment emphasis in today's health system disproportionately affects African American and Latino patients.

The committee speculated that the cost-containment emphasis in today's health system disproportionately affects African American and Latino patients. When doctors have limited resources, the most informed and assertive patients are likely to get preference. Cultural and linguistic barriers contribute to the skew, Smedley says. And even the most well-intended doctors sometimes act on unconscious stereotypes that may prompt them to prescribe some types of medication less often or stop short of recommending surgery.

In a book review in the *New England Journal of Medicine*, health outcomes researcher Peter Bach worried that the next step would be to threaten doctors with civil rights violations, rather than encouraging them to focus on improving the quality of care in underserved populations. In his own research, Bach, a Memorial Sloan Kettering Cancer Center physician, has identified differences in treatment as a core reason for survival differences between blacks and whites with cancer.

Sally Satel, a practicing psychiatrist and resident scholar at the American Enterprise Institute in Washington, D.C., says the Institute of Medicine's allegations of racism in the medical system are impossible to prove or disprove. The committee relied mainly on retrospective studies and therefore didn't have enough information to really understand differences in care, she says. More importantly, Satel asked, "Why focus on it? I think it's a huge distraction from the most important redress. The basic problems are economics and health literacy." Public health programs should be teaching people about wellness through grassroots programs in churches and community centers, she says, and medical savings accounts or more public health clinics might ease economic access.

Despite such criticism, the American Medical Association has now launched programs to teach its members about health care disparities, provide cultural training, create standards for treatment, and reach out to patients more effectively. The association also has encouraged race-based data collection in order to identify disparities and monitor progress against them. Separately, in March 2003, Aetna announced a program to measure use of its services by race, ethnicity and primary language. The insurer also said it would address the cultural competency of its physician network.

More attention to the ways that societal structures reinforce health disparities would be a welcome change, Nevarez says. It's not only Latinos, African Americans and Native Americans who would benefit, she emphasizes. Whites suffer from societal racism, too—in their hearts, their pocketbooks and their own health status, she says. Pointing to the high rates of hospitalization among black children with asthma and untreated tuberculosis in immigrant communities, she wonders, what is it in urban air that makes it hard to breathe? Why haven't Americans made it a priority to screen for tuberculosis, which observes no social barriers? "In some ways, poor people and people of color are the canaries in the coal mine," Nevarez says.

10

The Health Care System Is Not Racist

Sally Satel

Sally Satel is the staff psychiatrist at the Oasis Clinic in Washington, D.C., a resident scholar at the conservative think tank American Enterprise Institute, and the author of PC, M.D.: How Political Correctness Is Corrupting Medicine.

There is little evidence to prove that racism affects the quality of health care in minority communities. While some blacks, Hispanics, and Native Americans might not receive the highest quality health care, it is the result of physicians who work in minority communities having less access to expensive diagnostic equipment. These doctors are also less likely to recommend specialists to treat specific diseases. Critics should honor these urban physicians and realize that it is economics, not racism, that has created the problem. Financial incentives to draw well-trained doctors to minority neighborhoods would do much to eliminate the disparity in American health care.

At a certain point, it became possible to take a snapshot of America's health, complete with vivid details and statistical portraits. Among other things, the snapshot revealed that blacks and whites experience different rates of diabetes, stroke, some cancers and other conditions—and different rates of diagnosis and treatment. And the reason? Plausible answers easily come to mind: genetics, discrepancies in insurance cover-

Sally Satel, "A Case of Colorblind Care," *www.aei.org*, August 6, 2004. Copyright © 2004 Dow Jones & Company, Ltd. Reprinted with permission of *The Wall Street Journal* and the author.

age, the availability of medical care and varying patient attitudes toward it. Two years ago [2002], another reason was added: racism.

It was then that the Institute of Medicine (IOM) published "Unequal Treatment," a much-heralded report arguing that doctors—acting deliberately or unconsciously—were giving their minority patients inferior care. The notion that doctors (and thus the workings of the entire health-care system) commit "bias," "prejudice" and "stereotyping"—as the IOM report put it—is now conventional wisdom at many medical schools, philanthropies and health agencies. The Web site of the American Medical Association cites "discrimination at the individual patient-provider level" as a cause of health-care disparities. Introducing a health bill [in 2003] . . . Sen. Tom Daschle cited the need to correct doctors' "bias," "stereotyping" and "discrimination."

Skeptics of the biased-doctor model, and I count myself among them, do not dispute the troubling existence of a health gap. But we argue that the examining room is not the place to look for its origins. This is not to suggest that doctor-patient relationships are free of clinical uncertainty and miscommunication; they are not. But their relative importance is probably modest and remains hard to gauge, especially when compared with access to care and quality of care—both of which have undisputed and sizable effects.

This argument just got a big boost from researchers at Manhattan's Memorial Sloan-Kettering Cancer Center and the Center for the Study of Health Care Change in Washington. They showed that white and black patients, on average, do not even visit the same population of physicians—making the idea of preferential treatment by individual doctors a far less compelling explanation for disparities in health. They show, too, that a higher proportion of the doctors that black patients tend to see may not be in a position to provide optimal care.

Qualifications Differ

The dramatic finding, published [in August 2004] in the *New England Journal of Medicine*, should incite a fundamental shift in thinking. Whether it actually does that is another matter, so entrenched are the pieties about America's racist inclinations.

The research team, led by Dr. Peter Bach, examined more than 150,000 visits by black and white Medicare recipients to 4,355 primary-care physicians nationwide in 2001. It found that the vast majority of visits by black patients were made to a small group of physicians—80 percent of their visits were made to 22 percent of all the physicians in the study. Is it possible, the researchers asked, that doctors who disproportionately treat black patients are different from other doctors? Do their clinical qualifications and their resources differ?

> *Physicians of any race who disproportionately treat African-American patients . . . were less likely to have passed a demanding certification exam in their specialty than the physicians treating white patients.*

The answer is yes. Physicians of any race who disproportionately treat African-American patients, the study notes, were less likely to have passed a demanding certification exam in their specialty than the physicians treating white patients. More important, they were more likely to answer "not always" when asked whether they had access to high-quality colleagues—specialists to whom they could refer their patients (e.g., cardiologists, gastroenterologists), or to nonemergency hospital services, diagnostic imaging and ancillary services such as home health aid.

These patterns reflect geographic distribution. Primary-care physicians who lack board certification and who encounter obstacles to specialized services are more likely to practice in areas where blacks receive their care—namely, poorer neighborhoods, as measured by the median income.

Dr. Bach and his colleagues suggest that these differences play a considerable role in racial disparities in health care and health status. They make a connection between well-established facts: that physicians who are not board certified are (a) less likely to follow screening recommendations and (b) more likely to manage symptoms rather than pursue diagnosis. Thus rates of screening for breast and cervical cancer or high blood pressure are lower among black patients than white, and black patients are more likely to receive a diagnosis when their diseases are at an advanced stage. Limited access to specialty services similarly put black patients at a disadvantage.

The Bach study is the first to examine physicians' access to specialty care and nonemergency hospital admissions in light of the race of the patients they treat. As for the notion that the capacities of doctors who treat black patients may account for some part of the health gap, earlier evidence for it has been hiding in plain sight.

Physicians working for managed-care plans in which black patients were heavily enrolled provided lower-quality care to all patients.

For example, a 2002 study in the *Journal of the American Medical Association* found that physicians working for managed-care plans in which black patients were heavily enrolled provided lower-quality care to all patients. A report in the *American Journal of Public Health* in 2000 found that black patients undergoing cardiovascular surgery had poorer access to high-quality surgeons. Similarly, Dartmouth researchers have shown that African-Americans tend to live in areas or seek care in regions where the quality for all patients, black and white, is at a lower level.

It is important to recognize that many of the physicians working in black communities are hardworking, committed individuals who make considerable financial sacrifices to serve their patients. As Dr. Bach's team notes, they deliver more charity care than doctors who mostly treat white patients and derive a higher volume of their practice revenue from Medicaid, a program whose fees are notoriously low. They are often solo practitioners who scramble to make good referrals for their patients but who are stymied by a dearth of well-trained colleagues and by limited entrée to professional networks with advanced diagnostic techniques.

It is long past time to put aside the incendiary claim that racism plays a meaningful role in the health status of African-Americans. The health gap is assuredly real. But growing evidence suggests that the most promising course is to get well-trained doctors into low-income and rural neighborhoods and enable them to provide the best care for their patients—something they will do, it somehow needs to be said, without prejudice.

11

Christians Face Persecution in America

David Limbaugh, as interviewed by Kathryn Jean Lopez

David Limbaugh is a lawyer, syndicated columnist, and author of Persecution: How Liberals Are Waging War Against Christianity. *Kathryn Jean Lopez is an award-winning opinion journalist, editor of* National Review Online, *and an associate editor at* National Review. *She has appeared on CNN, the Fox News Channel, and MSNBC.*

Editor's Note: The following article is taken from an interview by Kathryn Jean Lopez with David Limbaugh, who discusses topics from his book Persecution: How Liberals Are Waging War Against Christianity.

There is a war against Christians in the United States today. In schools, courthouses, and public squares, Christians are forced to hide symbols of their faith for fear of upsetting secular humanists who are biased against religious expression. Discussions of the Christian influence on American history and society have been purged from schoolbooks while a secular agenda of homosexual rights and political correctness has been promoted across the nation. Christians must stand together against the secular forces that wish to create a society in which antireligious values are promoted over the core beliefs of most Americans. Christians are not asking the government to endorse their religion, but also expect the government not to endorse competing, secular values.

K ATHRYN JEAN LOPEZ: Isn't a little much to say there's a war against Christianity in the U.S? Especially when we are in an actual war against terrorism?

Various groups are working to scrub away Christianity from the public square and to reduce religious liberty for Christians.

DAVID LIMBAUGH: Well, I certainly don't mean to diminish the actual war on terrorism. The "war" I describe in my book is, of course, a very different kind of war—more along the lines of the culture war. I believe I make a compelling case in my book that various groups are working to scrub away Christianity from the public square and to reduce religious liberty for Christians. Nothing in the Constitution limits our First Amendment freedoms of speech, religion, and association to our homes and churches. That is, we do not forfeit those freedoms when we enter government property, public schools, or the public square. The secularists' efforts to confine Christian religious liberty to our homes and churches is a disturbing development. . . .

LOPEZ: In what area are Christians most persistently persecuted?

LIMBAUGH: The attack against Christians is occurring in many areas, including public education, the universities, the public square, government property and institutions, the mainstream media, Hollywood, the courts, and even the private sector and in our churches. I would say that the majority of examples can be found in the public schools, though the public square is a close second. The humanists have been targeting our children for more than a century. . . . Charles F. Potter, who wrote *Humanism: A New Religion*, believed that the key to controlling the culture was to indoctrinate the children—in public schools. He wrote, "Education is thus a most powerful ally of Humanism, and every American public school is a school of Humanism. What can the theistic Sunday-schools, meeting for an hour once a week, and teaching only a fraction of the children, do to stem the tide of a five-day program of humanistic teaching?" In Chapters Three and Four [of my book] I ... proceed to document the inroads the humanists have made in controlling our public-school curriculum, which clearly impart anti-Christian values and endorse other values-based ideas, from Secular Humanism, to New Age to Native Spirituality and Islam. Those clamoring for a strict separation of church and state never raise a hand of objection to the government's endorsement of this non-Christian, values-laden instruction.

LOPEZ: Is it just Christianity?

LIMBAUGH: Of course there is a bias against religion generically, but the overwhelming majority of discrimination in our culture is targeted at Christians and Christianity. The most likely reason is that Christianity is perceived as the majority religion and its absolute standards of right and wrong interfere with the advancement of the radical secularist agenda, the homosexual lobby, the feminist movement, and other politically correct nostrums.

LOPEZ: What is the most egregious example of persecution?

LIMBAUGH: I document hundreds if not thousands of cases of discrimination against Christians, backed up by almost 800 footnotes. It is difficult for me to choose the most egregious example because there are so many outrageous ones. Some are just plain silly—but not humorous because they are actual events in the real world. One that sticks out in my mind as an example of the utter extremism and disproportion of the secularists occurred with the Madison, Wisconsin Metro System. Each month this government entity placed a picture of some public figure on its bus pass. One month it used Martin Luther King Jr. and another, Elvis Presley, another the inventor of the Internet, Tim Berners-Lee. . . . But when it decided to use Mother Teresa, the Freedom From Religion Foundation [FFRF] went ballistic, saying it was an impermissible intermingling of government and religion. "Religious figures," said FFRF president Annie Laurie Gaylor, "do not belong on monthly passes of publicly owned transportation facilities." Plus, according to Gaylor, the selection would be an "insult" to women's rights, since she "campaigned stridently throughout her life at every opportunity against access to contraception, sterilization and abortion for anyone."

LOPEZ: How is anti-Christian persecution playing out in the firestorm over [director] Mel Gibson's *Passion* [movie about the crucifixion of Jesus]?

LIMBAUGH: The anti-Christian influence is clearly seen in the controversy over Mel Gibson's *Passion*. How ironic that when a man tries to stay true to the Biblical and sacred texts in relating the culminating events in the life of the most important man to have ever lived, he is castigated as an anti-Semite and his breathtaking film has difficulty finding a Hollywood producer. Yet when the culture produces plays that blasphemously depict Christ as a homosexual (*Corpus Christi*), or movies that show him as a sinner (*The Last Temptation of Christ*), or art that dips the crucifix into a vat of urine or spreads with cow dung images of the Virgin Mary, they are celebrated by the elites. The secularists utter not a word in protest of the offensive nature of these works, nor of the state's endorsement of their anti-Christian themes.

References to Christianity and to America's Christian heritage have been deliberately excised from most public school textbooks.

Purging Religion from Public Schools

LOPEZ: Is Christianity really being "excised" from public school?

LIMBAUGH: Yes, references to Christianity and to America's Christian heritage have been deliberately excised from most public school textbooks. As I detail in Chapter Three, New York University psychology professor Paul Vitz conducted extensive research documenting the purging of religion—primarily the Christian religion—from public schools. He studied 60 social-studies texts used in some 87 percent of public schools and determined that the Christian influence on our culture was completely ignored. "There is not one story or article in all these books in which the central motivation or major content is connected to Judeo-Christian religion. . . .None of the books covering grades one through four contains one word referring to any religious activity in contemporary American life," wrote Vitz. In addition, as I demonstrate in Chapters One and Two, Christian freedom and speech are under assault. In the name of promoting freedom of religion through a strict enforcement of "separation of church and state" the schools are suppressing the free exercise rights of students. Voluntary student Christian religious expression is suppressed. There is nothing in the Constitution, by the way, that limits the freedom of religion (or speech) to the privacy of our homes and the churches. As I said, we do not forfeit our religious freedoms when we enter government property, public schools or the public square.

LOPEZ: How pernicious is K-12 anti-Christian persecution?

LIMBAUGH: The examples of anti-Christian discrimination in K-12 and the endorsement of opposing worldviews is so widespread that I devoted four chapters to it. And before the editing process began I had almost twice the material in this section, but had to cut it down to the make the book manageable. The examples are voluminous and reveal that the humanists have been largely successful in achieving their goal of taking over the public schools. From "comprehensive" sex education, to Western and Christian-trashing multiculturalism to history revisionism to death education, to the self-esteem movement, to undermining parental values, to New Age values to Fuzzy Math and Inventive Spelling—these "educational" ideas are just too bizarre to be justified on an academic basis. They have to be born of some ideological agenda. And the failure of public education can be traced directly to this nonsense. No amount of federal money is going to change this until parents wake up to the insanity that is pervading the schools.

We need to stop the bleeding, not by overreacting, but by standing up against the chilling, oppressive and intimidating nature of political correctness and the secular humanist forces in our culture.

LOPEZ: Do Christians know all of this is going on?

Raising Awareness

LIMBAUGH: Unfortunately, many Christians do not seem to be fully aware that they are under attack, which is the primary reason for this book. It is intended to be a clarion call to Christians, jolting them out of their complacency, alerting them—if they don't already realize it—that they are the primary targets in a culture war. I believe the evidence I've adduced in the book is overwhelming. While my liberal critics on some of the talk shows have charged that my examples are merely anecdotal, I respond that examples, by themselves, or in small groups, are by definition anecdotal. But at some point—and we've greatly exceeded that point here—the sheer number and variety of the attacks constitutes evidence of a systematic and comprehensive, if not overtly conspiratorial, assault on Christianity and Christian freedom. I'm not some sensationalist or alarmist, suggesting that we've passed the point of no return or that we've lost all our religious freedoms. In fact, I parted company with many of my conservative Christian friends when I supported Alabama Chief Justice Roy Moore until he violated the federal court order. I argued that he should work within the system, no matter how flawed or erroneous the higher courts' decisions on the Establishment Clause. Some readers objected that the federal court's order was itself unlawful and thus must be disobeyed. Well, we disagree with a lot of decisions the courts make, but unless we're prepared for another revolution or full-blown anarchy I think we've got an obligation to obey the law. If I thought our entire library of Christian religious liberties had been eviscerated I too would be advocating drastic action. But we still have the liberty to worship as we choose in our churches and in private. The assault is primarily going on in the public sector. If we don't stop it at this point, it will certainly continue and we will lose our liberties. But we're not there yet—and we need to stop the bleeding, not by overreacting, but by standing up against the chilling, oppressive and intimidating nature of political correctness and the secular humanist forces in our culture.

LOPEZ: If there were medals to be awarded for bravery in this "war" who'd be the first you'd want to see get one?

LIMBAUGH: Part of the defense of the faith, both in the culture and the courts, requires the courage to stand up to the opposition. There are many people on the frontlines in this battle, such as all the Christian public-interest law firms fighting on a county-by-county basis throughout the United States to vindicate religious liberty. But if I had to choose one person who is standing up for the faith publicly, notwithstanding the endless assaults, it would be President George W. Bush. He has unapologetically declared his allegiance to Christ and his reliance on Him for guidance in governance. All Bush has to do is invoke the concepts of good and evil and he's castigated as a simplistic Christian cowboy, intolerant and dangerous to society and to the world. But when he invokes God he incurs the wrath of the entire secular left, from [*New York Times* columnist] Maureen Dowd to [president of People for The American Way] Barry Lynn. But he doesn't back down. [Former] Attorney General John Ashcroft is a close second.

LOPEZ: Do you have a plan of action for Christians?

As Christians, in the legal arena, we simply want an equal seat at the table of religious liberty.

LIMBAUGH: I have no magical solution for these problems, other than to raise awareness and call Christians—and all other lovers of liberty—to action. Christians, contrary to popular myth, do not want to establish a theocracy. We don't even necessarily want the government to endorse religion. I would say that the Establishment Clause certainly doesn't require a complete divorce of government and religion. The very day after the first Congress in 1789 passed the First Amendment, it declared a national day of prayer and thanksgiving. Chief Justice Story later wrote that there was never any intention by the framers to prevent the government from endorsing, in some respects, the Christian religion. Though the Constitution doesn't require the government to stay wholly out of religion, as a policy matter, in this pluralistic society, I have no problem with the government attempting to stay neutral on religion. But nature abhors a vacuum and so do the secularists. So the least we can ask for is fair play—no overt endorsement of Christianity, fine; but don't endorse competing values either. The assault on Christianity is multifaceted and therefore requires a multifaceted response. We need to fight to restore Biblical theology and moral rectitude to our churches and church governing hierarchies. We need to fight for the hearts of people in our culture. We need to fight the education establishment by opposing its monopoly on education and its militant advancement of secular humanist values and purging of Christianity. This means that we should support the home school and school choice movements. We must continue to fight in the courts and to elect presidents who will appoint, and Senators who will confirm, constitutionalist judges. And we need to keep our voices heard in the media as well. And we must couch this battle primarily in terms of religious freedom. As Christians, in the legal arena, we simply want an equal seat at the table of religious liberty. But at the level of our culture, we must understand that our freedoms are an outgrowth of our Judeo-Christian traditions. Our Christian roots make clear that it is no accident that America is the freest and most prosperous nation in the history of the world—which is why the secularists have such a compelling interest to revise history and conceal the Christian influence. No matter how ingeniously crafted the Constitution was, the framers warned that it was made only for a moral and religious people. Which means that if we abandon our absolute standards of right and wrong—the Judeo-Christian ethic—in the interest of modern day notions of tolerance and diversity, we'll remove the foundation upon which our liberties are built. Maybe not immediately, but within a few generations or so, our liberties will eventually implode. As that time approaches, it will be too late for alarmism. So let's get into the fight now, while there is still time.

12

Atheists Suffer Discrimination in the United States

Eddie Tabash

Eddie Tabash is a member of the board of directors of the Council for Secular Humanism and is a constitutional lawyer in Beverly Hills, California.

Atheists in the United States face open discrimination if not blatant hostility from the general public. As a result, those who do not believe in God or religion are often afraid to express their viewpoint. To counter this discrimination, atheists need to run for political office. As one of the most despised minorities in America today, it is imperative that atheists elect politicians who will hold the line against overwhelming religious forces. At a time when nearly three-quarters of all Americans want to legalize prayer in public schools, atheists will not achieve full equality under the law without electing nonbelievers to political office.

One test of whether a minority group's struggle for equality is a civil rights issue is whether majority attitudes toward that minority reflect unreasonable prejudice or a desire to deny full legal rights to its members. By this standard, atheists' efforts to achieve legal and social equality indeed constitute a civil rights movement. Consider that, in 1958, a Gallup poll revealed that 53 percent of American citizens would vote against a Black candidate for president on grounds of race alone. In a 1999 Gallup poll, that figure had declined to 4

Eddie Tabash, "Atheism is Indeed A Civil Rights Issue," *Free Inquiry*, vol. 24, June-July 2004. Copyright 2004 Council for Democratic and Secular Humanism, Inc. Reproduced by permission.

percent. That same 1999 Gallup poll revealed that a larger percentage of American citizens, 49 percent, would vote against an atheist *on grounds of atheism alone* than would vote against someone for any other reason. Even though this is the lowest comparative percentage of people who said they would vote against someone just for being a nonbeliever, in absolute numbers, it is still a higher percentage than is applicable to any other historically disfavored group.

Given current attitudes, new laws that overtly discriminate against atheists would pass easily, and any such existing laws would eagerly be enforced.

Given current attitudes, new laws that overtly discriminate against atheists would pass easily, and any such existing laws would eagerly be enforced—save only for the United States Supreme Court, which has held consistently since 1947 that no branch of government can favor believers over nonbelievers. Enlightened as this position may be, it has never enjoyed majority support. Quite to the contrary, each time the Supreme Court, indeed any court, has struck down government preference for religion over nonbelief, an overwhelming majority of the public has opposed the decision in question.

Ever since the famous Supreme Court rulings of 1962 and 1963 that ended teacher-led prayer and Bible readings in public schools, in poll after poll Americans have favored returning government sponsored prayer to public schools by a *minimum* margin of 69 percent to 27 percent. In many surveys, the percentage favoring restoration of school prayer exceeds 75 percent.

In other words, an overwhelming majority of Americans rejects the offer of fairness that atheists and secular humanists have always proposed. We don't want government to favor us over others; we just want government to be neutral, so that both believers and nonbelievers will be equal before the law.

We want government to stay out of the God controversy, so that the official structure of society equally embraces both believers and nonbelievers. We want government to be silent on the question of God's existence and on matters of worship. Even a moderate conservative like [former] U.S. Supreme Court Justice Sandra Day O'Connor has endorsed this position, asserting that the First Amendment prohibits all branches of government from treating people differently based upon "the God or gods they worship or don't worship.". . .

Nonbelievers are the most unjustly despised minority in the United States today.

Nonbelievers Are Loathed

Since the majority in our nation regards nonbelievers with disdain and craves an end to government neutrality between religion and nonbelief, the struggle of atheists in the United States is indeed a civil rights issue. But that's not the worst of it.

Mainstream Americans don't simply reject atheism. Far too many of them also revile atheists, secular humanists, and other unbelievers as persons. In reflecting upon my own narrow loss in my 2000 bid for a seat in the California legislature, I have written that nonbelievers are the most unjustly despised minority in the United States today.

History and current events confirm how sharply nonbelievers are loathed. Consider the torrent of hatred today directed toward Michael Newdow, the courageous plaintiff in the effort to remove "under God" from the Pledge of Allegiance that public school children are expected to recite. Far from being unusual, the negative public response toward Newdow *typifies* the rage with which most Americans respond when anyone from our community demands that official government pronouncements be as equally inclusive of us as they are of everyone else.

Or consider a historical example. In February 1964, when the landmark Civil Rights Act was being debated in Congress, the House of Representatives passed a measure by a vote of 137 to 98 that *explicitly excluded atheists* from protection under the new law that would otherwise abolish employment discrimination. Fortunately, the measure failed in the Senate. Still, just forty years ago, the same House of Representatives that declared it illegal to engage in employment discrimination against African Americans was willing to give employers free rein to go on discriminating against people who didn't believe in God.

I submit that bigotry against a person just because that individual rejects unproven supernatural claims is every bit as destructive of the quest for a just and enlightened society as is bigotry against someone on grounds of race or ethnicity.

To the extent that a clear majority of Americans, let alone an overwhelming majority, *wants* government at all levels to officially favor religion over nonbelief—to the extent that more Americans still view atheism as a disqualifying characteristic in a political candidate than they do any other factor—I submit that we nonbelievers are in just as much danger of suffering open discrimination as is the gay community. Even though there have not yet been any notable physical attacks on atheists—just for being atheists—discrimination does not have to be accompanied by overt violence in order to pose a grave threat to a minority group's struggle for full equality. Further, if President Bush succeeds in restructuring the Supreme Court so as to create a majority willing to nullify church-state separation, open discrimination against atheists and secular humanists may become the active and enforceable law of the land.

Accordingly, the efforts of atheists, secular humanists, and other nonbelievers to secure and preserve their equality before the law is every bit as much a civil rights struggle as is that of the gay rights movement.

Should Atheists Elect Their Own?

One of the most important advances members of any unjustly despised minority can make is to begin electing members of their own community to political office. Consider how pathetically contemporary politicians pander to religion—for example, when every United States senator gathered on the Capitol steps to support "under God" in the Pledge of Allegiance after the initial Ninth Circuit finding favorable to Newdow was announced [in March 2004]. Clearly our best protection against legislation hostile to nonbelievers would be to get some atheists elected to Congress and state legislatures. . . .

> *Since the mood of the country is so antagonistic toward atheists, our own quest to secure and preserve equality before the law is clearly a civil rights issue.*

Given the dearth of nonbelievers currently holding significant political office in the United States, when one of our colleagues in freethought makes a bid for office and has a significant chance of winning, we should try to give that candidate our support even if we do not agree with him or her on every issue. We nonbelievers can be a contentious lot, often withholding our backing from anyone with whom we disagree on even just one issue. As a practical matter, we will never find a candidate with whom we agree on everything. My suggestion, then, is for atheists and secular humanists to try to give a viable candidate from our own community greater leeway on topics not directly germane to the equal rights of nonbelievers and church-state separation. Each of us should try to support that candidate, unless he or she holds a position on some issue that violates one of our core individual beliefs.

The gay community, women, African Americans, and other minority groups have learned the importance of civil rights activism, and of electing their own to political office. Since the mood of the country is so antagonistic toward atheists, our own quest to secure and preserve equality before the law is clearly a civil rights issue. As such, just like any other unjustly despised minority, we must learn how to elect a number of our own to the halls of power.

Organizations to Contact

American Atheists
PO Box 5733, Parsippany, NJ   07054-6733
Phone: 908-276-7300 • Fax: 908-276-7402
Email: info@atheists.org
Web site: www.atheists.org

American Atheists is a nonprofit educational organization that provides information about the atheist philosophy and state-church separation issues. The organization publishes the magazine *American Atheist*, the e-mail newsletter *AANEWS*, and the blog NoGodBlog.com.

American Enterprise Institute (AEI)
1150 Seventeenth St. NW, Washington, DC   20036
Phone: 202-862-5800 • Fax: 202-862-7177
Email: webmaster@aei.org
Web site: www.aei.org

The American Enterprise Institute is a conservative think tank dedicated to limited government, private enterprise, and a strong foreign policy and national defense. AEI publishes op-eds, newsletters, and papers, as well as speeches, government testimony, and books.

Cato Institute
1000 Massachusetts Ave. NW, Washington, DC   20001-5403
Phone (202) 842-0200 • Fax (202) 842-3490
Email: jblock@cato.org
Web site: www.cato.org

The Cato Institute is a nonprofit libertarian public policy research foundation headquartered in Washington, D.C. It seeks to broaden the parameters of public policy debate to allow consideration of the traditional American principles of limited government, individual liberty, free markets, and peace. The institute researches issues in the media and provides commentary for magazines, newspapers, and news programs.

Congress on Racial Equality (CORE)
817 Broadway, New York, NY   10003
Phone: 212-598-4000 • Fax: 212-598-4141
Email: core@core-online.org
Web site: www.core-online.org

CORE is the third-oldest civil rights group in the United States, and the only one championing conservative values. Under the slogan of "Truth! Logic! & Courage!," CORE's aim is to bring about equality for all people regardless of race, creed, sex, age, disability, religion, or ethnic background. The group publishes press releases and featured articles on its Web site along with the on-line newsletter the *Correlator*.

Council for Secular Humanism
PO Box 664, Amherst, NY   14226-0664
Phone: 716-636-7571 • Fax: 716-636-1733
E-mail: info@secularhumanism.org
Web site: www.secularhumanism.org

The Council for Secular Humanism serves the needs of nonreligious people by fostering human enrichment with rational inquiry, ethical values, and human development through the advancement of secular humanism. To promote secular humanist principles to the public, media, and policy makers, the council sponsors programs and organizes meetings and other group activities. The organization publishes the magazine *Free Inquiry*, the *Secular Humanist Bulletin* newsletter, and books and pamphlets promoting secular humanism.

The Heritage Foundation
214 Massachusetts Ave. NE, Washington, DC   20002
Phone: 202-546-4400 • Fax: 202-544-2260
Email: pubs@heritage.org
Web site: www.heritage.org

The Heritage Foundation is a conservative public policy research institute that supports the principles of free enterprise and limited federal government interference in campaign financing and other election matters. Its many publications include the monthly *Policy Review* and position papers concerning terrorism, election reform, and constitutional issues.

Hudson Institute

1015 Eighteenth St. NW, Suite 300, Washington, DC 20036
Phone: 202-223-7770 • Fax: 202-223-8537
Email: info@hudsondc.org
Website: www.hudson.org/

The Hudson Institute is a conservative think tank that supplies research, books, and policy ideas to leaders in communities, businesses, nonprofit organizations, and governments. The institute is committed to free markets and individual responsibility, confidence in the power of technology to assist progress, respect for the importance of culture and religion in human affairs, and determination to preserve America's national security. It publishes books, articles, and reports, which are available on its Web site.

Institute for Women's Policy Research (IWPR)

1707 L St. NW, Suite 750, Washington, DC 20036
Phone: 202-785-5100 • Fax: 202-833-4362
E-mail: iwpr@iwpr.org
Web Site: www.iwpr.org

The Institute for Women's Policy Research is a scientific research organization dedicated to informing and stimulating the debate on public policy issues of critical importance to women and their families. IWPR focuses on issues of poverty and welfare, employment and earnings, work and family issues, health and safety, and women's civic and political participation. Its publications include briefing papers and reports such as *The Status of Women in the States* and *The Ties That Bind: Women's Public Vision for Politics, Religion, and Civil Society.*

National Organization for Women (NOW)

1100 H St. NW, 3rd Fl., Washington, DC   20005
Phone: 202-628-8NOW (8669) • Fax: 202-785-8576
Email: now@now.org
Web site: www.now.org

The National Organization for Women is the largest organization of feminist activists in the United States with five hundred thousand contributing members and 550 chapters in all fifty states and the District of Columbia. Since its founding in 1966, NOW's goal has been to bring about equality for all women; to eliminate discrimination and harassment in the workplace; to secure abortion, birth control, and reproductive rights for all women; and to end all forms of violence against women. The organization publishes press releases and a biannual newsletter, *NOW Times*.

National Urban League

120 Wall St., 8th Fl., New York, NY   10005
Phone: 212-558-5300
Email: info@nul.org
Web site: www.nul.org

The National Urban League is the nation's oldest and largest community-based movement devoted to helping African Americans secure economic self-reliance, parity, power, and civil rights. There are more than one hundred local affiliates of the National Urban League located in thirty-five states and the District of Columbia providing direct services to more than 2 million people nationwide through programs, advocacy, and research. The group publishes books, magazines, and columns, including *The State of Black America*, the *Opportunity Journal*, *Urban Influence*, and the weekly syndicated "To Be Equal" column.

United for a Fair Economy (UFE)

29 Winter St., Boston, MA   02108
Phone: 617-423-2148 • Fax: 617-423-0191

Email: info@faireconomy.org
Website: www.faireconomy.org

United for a Fair Economy is a national nonpartisan organization founded to raise awareness about the issue of concentrated wealth and power that members believe undermines the economy, corrupts democracy, deepens the racial divide, and tears communities apart. UFE publishes books such as *The Wealth Inequality Reader* and *Greed and Good: Understanding and Overcoming the Inequality That Limits Our Lives.* Reports, opinion pieces, and policy papers are available on its Web site.

Young America's Foundation (YAF)

F. M. Kirby Freedom Center, Herndon, VA   20170
Phone: 800-USA-1776 • Fax: 703-318-9122
Email: yaf@yaf.org
web address: www.yaf.org

Young America's Foundation is a conservative organization committed to ensuring that increasing numbers of young Americans understand the ideas of individual freedom, a strong national defense, free enterprise, and traditional values. The group accomplishes its mission by providing conferences, seminars, educational materials, internships, and speakers to young people across the country. YAF also publishes the journal *Libertas* three times a year.

Bibliography

Books

Ellen Ann Andersen	*Out of the Closets and into the Courts: Legal Opportunity Structure and Gay Rights Litigation.* Ann Arbor: University of Michigan Press, 2005.
Andrew Barlow	*Between Fear and Hope: Globalization and Race in the United States.* Lanham, MD: Rowman & Littlefield, 2003.
Eduardo Bonilla-Silva	*Racism Without Racists: Color-Blind Racism and the Persistence of Racial Inequality in the United States.* Lanham, MD: Rowman & Littlefield, 2003.
Kingsley R. Browne	*Biology at Work: Rethinking Sexual Equality.* New Brunswick, NJ: Rutgers University Press, 2002.
Michael Brown et al.	*Whitewashing Race: The Myth of a Colorblind Society.* Berkeley and Los Angeles: University of California Press, 2003.
Dalton Conley	*Being Black, Being in the Red: Race, Wealth and Social Policy in America.* Berkeley and Los Angeles: University of California Press, 1999.

Derek H. Davis and Barry Hankins, eds. — *New Religious Movements and Religious Liberty in America.* Waco, TX: Baylor University Press, 2003.

Ashley Doane — *Whiteout: The Continuing Significance of Racism.* New York: Routledge, 2003.

Nicholas Everitt — *The Non-Existence of God.* New York: Routledge, 2004.

Joe Feagin — *White Men on Race.* Boston: Beacon Press, 2003.

Andrew Hacker — *Two Nations Black and White: Separate, Hostile and Unequal.* New York: Ballantine, 1992.

H.N. Hirsch, ed. — *The Future of Gay Rights in America.* New York: Routledge, 2005.

Chrys Ingraham — *Thinking Straight: The Power, the Promise, and the Paradox of Heterosexuality.* New York: Routledge, 2005.

Jonathan Kozol — *The Shame of the Nation: The Restoration of Apartheid Schooling in America.* New York: Crown, 2005.

David Limbaugh — *Persecution: How Liberals Are Waging War Against Christianity.* Washington, DC: Regnery, 2003.

Alister McGrath — *The Twilight of Atheism: The Rise and Fall of Disbelief in the Modern World.* New York: Doubleday, 2004.

David Moats — *Civil Wars: A Battle for Gay Marriage.* Orlando, FL: Harcourt, 2004.

Sam Parkhouse — *Powerful Women: Dancing on the Glass Ceiling.* Chichester, UK: Wiley, 2001.

Sue V. Rosser — *The Science Glass Ceiling: Academic Women Scientists and the Struggle to Succeed.* New York: Routledge, 2004.

Stephen Thernstrom and Abigail Thernstrom — *America in Black and White: One Nation Indivisible.* New York: Simon and Schuster, 1997.

Sue Thomas and Clyde Wilcox, eds. — *Women and Elective Office: Past, Present, and Future.* Oxford: Oxford University Press, 2005.

Linda Wirth — *Breaking Through the Glass Ceiling: Women in Management.* Geneva, Switzerland: International Labour Office, 2001.

Periodicals

Gary S. Becker — "How to Level the Playing Field for Young Black Men," *Business Week*, August 4, 2003.

Stephen L. Carter — "Hope Deferred: Christians Are Uniquely Positioned to Further Racial Equality," *Christianity Today*, July 2004.

Marci A. Hamilton — "Room for Religion; What's Allowed on Government Property?" *Christian Century*, August 9, 2005.

Alphonso Jackson "It Really Is Black and White...", *Wall Street Journal*, April 19, 2005.

Njeri Jackson "Fathering Injustice: Racial Patriarchy and the Dismantling of Affirmative Action," *Western Journal of Black Studies*, Spring 2003.

Richard D. Kahlenberg *"Brown v. Board of Education*: A Civil Rights Milestone and Its Troubled Legacy," *American Prospect*, May 21, 2001.

Jeremy Leaming "Marriage Proposal: Religious Right, Political Allies Launch Crusade to Alter Constitution," *Church & State*, October 2003.

Paul E. Peterson "The Brown Irony: Racial Progress Eventually Came to Pass—Everywhere but in Public Schools," *Education Next*, Fall 2004.

Deb Price "Other Nations Point the Way to Marital Equality," *Detroit News*, May 16, 2005.

Franklin D. Raines "40 Acres and a Mortgage: Why Home Ownership Is Key to Achieving Racial Equality," *Sojourners*, September/October 2002.

John E. Roemer "Defending Equality of Opportunity," *Monist*, April 2003.

Ann Rostow — "Making Vows for Equality: Straight Couples like Tracy and Vivek Are Dedicating Their Weddings to the Fight for Equal Marriage Rights," *Advocate*, Sept 27, 2005.

Fred O. Smith Jr. — "Gendered Justice: Do Male and Female Judges Rule Differently on Questions of Gay Rights?" *Stanford Law Review*, May 2005.

Jay Tolson — "Divided, We Stand," *U.S. News & World Report*, August 8, 2005.

Kathie Uhrmacher — "Equality in Pay for Working Women Is Long Overdue," *Lincoln (NE) Journal Star*, April 19, 2005.

Sarah Wildman — "Faith-Based Equality: What Would Jesus Do, Indeed," *Advocate*, September 13, 2005.

Index

affirmative action, 26
African Americans
  gains made by, 7–8
  have equal opportunities,
    23–27
      con, 28–36
  health care system discrimi-
    nates against, 65–71
      con, 72–76
  homeownership by, 34–35
  income levels of, 31–33
  optimism of young, 25–26
  in politics, 7–8, 24–27
  in prison, 31
  unemployment among, 9,
    30–31
  workplace discrimination
    against, 8–9
  see also minorities
Albright, Madeleine, 50
American Atheists, 92
American Enterprise Institute
  (AEI), 92
Ashcroft, John, 84
Asian Americans, 39
  see also minorities
asset ownership
  barriers to, 29–33
  government commitment to,
    35–36
  homeownership, 34–35
asset transfers, 33
atheists, are discriminated against,
  86–91

Bach, Peter, 70, 74, 75, 76
Bradley, Bill, 19
Bush, George W.
  homeownership agenda of,
    34–35
  inaugural address by, 23

  losses for minorities under,
    29
  support of Christianity by,
    83–84
  tax cuts by, 21, 30, 31

capital gains taxes, 19
Carnegie, Andrew, 16
Cato Institute, 92–93
CEOs
  gender gap in, 8–9
  lack of qualified, 48–49
  salaries of, 20
children, affect of having on
  women's careers, 47–49
Christians, are persecuted in U.S.,
  77–85
Civil Rights Act of 1964, 38, 50,
  89
civil rights movement, 7, 24
Civil War, 7
college degrees, earned by
  women, 46–47, 48
compassionate conservatism, 29
Congress on Racial Equality
  (CORE), 93
Council for Secular Humanism,
  93
cultural war
  against atheists, 86–91
  against Christians in U.S.,
    77–85

Danko, William, 12
Declaration of Independence, 7
de Tocqueville, Alexis, 15–16
discrimination
  against atheists, 86–91
  against Christians, 77–85
  in health care system, 65–71
    con, 72–76